LOONS
HAVE LANDED!

BY TERRY CAMP

Edited by Peter Johnston

Copyright © 2007 Foxhound Books

Text design and cover design by Rhonda Scharlat Hughes.
Photos copyright as noted.

Mr. Camp welcomes inquiries, comments, and requests for speaking engagements. Please email him at tckom@charter.net for more information and to be informed of any future offerings.

ISBN 978-0-9794110-0-7

To my wife Katie, who inspires and encourages me to attempt things I wouldn't have dared tried if she weren't in my life, and to my children, Mackenzie, Madison, Joe—and, keeping with a baseball trade theme— our fourth child, a girl, who will be named at a later date.

Table of Contents

FOREWORD *by William Stavropoulos*   **7**

PART I: A DREAM COME TRUE?
   CHAPTER 1. The Call   **13**
   CHAPTER 2. We've Been Here Before   **19**
   CHAPTER 3. Tracking the Story   **31**

PART II: A MAN WITH A PLAN
   CHAPTER 4. The Leader Emerges   **47**
   CHAPTER 5. The Fast Lane   **57**
   CHAPTER 6. Now We Need a Stadium   **69**
   CHAPTER 7. No, No, *This* Year   **81**

PART III: IF YOU BUILD IT, WILL THEY COME?
   CHAPTER 8. What's in a Name (I)   **95**
   CHAPTER 9. Divorced by the Devil Rays   **109**
   CHAPTER 10. What's in a Name (II)   **123**
   CHAPTER 11: A Requiem in Battle Creek   **131**

PART IV: ROOT, ROOT, ROOT FOR THE HOME TEAM
   CHAPTER 12: What It Means to Us   **141**
   CHAPTER 13: The Thaw   **147**

APPENDIX: THE MIDWEST LEAGUE   **152**
ACKNOWLEDGEMENTS   **158**

Foreword

Bringing the Great Lakes Loons and the Dow Diamond to Midland, Michigan has been one of the most enjoyable and personally satisfying projects I've ever been involved with. It was also a wild ride, as Terry Camp explains in this delightful account of how the whole thing came together.

We all love baseball—you'd have to, to do something like this—but our real purpose was to improve the quality of life in our region with a new source of entertainment. We wanted to help create something that could serve as an economic spark for the region—something to help attract and hold the companies and talented people we depend on for our future prosperity.

So here we are. Every spring and summer we'll have about 70 home games to enjoy. The Dow Diamond is a year-round facility, and we look forward to hosting a whole range of events and attractions throughout the year. Beyond entertainment, the Michigan Baseball Foundation has a charitable purpose; profits from the stadium and the Loons will be put back into the community for youth activities.

The team and the stadium are set up as a self-sustaining venture, so this new feature of mid-Michigan life will be permanent: the Loons are here to stay. As you'll see, bringing this all together was very much a joint effort. If not for the hard work and generosity of many, many people—and a genuine desire on their part to bring something new and special to central Michigan—it would never have happened.

But it did, and I'd like to take this opportunity to acknowledge and thank some of the people who made it possible. First of all, thanks go to the people and organizations whose encouragement and financial support enabled the project to get off the ground: Margaret Ann (Ranny) Riecker, Herbert H. and Grace A. Dow Foundation; Alan Ott, Rollin M. Gerstacker Foundation; Bobbie Arnold, Charles J. Strosacker Foundation; Andrew Liveris, Dow Chemical Foundation; Stephanie Burns, Dow Corning Corporation; and Linda Stavropoulos, William and Linda Stavropoulos Foundation.

The Dow Chemical Company has been extremely supportive of this venture from the beginning. For everything from the land the stadium sits on, to financial support, to the expertise and dedication that managed to put a stadium in place in less than one year, I'd like to extend a special thank-you to Andrew Liveris, Michael Hayes, Peyman Zand, Arnold Allemang, Fred Eddy, Greg Grocholski, and John Bartos.

Enormous help and guidance, on an ongoing basis, is provided by the board of directors of the Michigan Baseball Foundation: in addition to Mike Hayes and John Bartos, the directors are Dom Monastiere, Jenée Velasquez, Frank Brod, Marty McGuire, Bill Weiderman, Abbe Mulders, Arnold Allemang, Eric Gilbertson, and Sue Kaltenbach.

Finally, from all these people and myself, our heartfelt thanks to all the people of central Michigan for their support and enthusiasm. May you enjoy the games as much as we've enjoyed bringing them here. Go Loons!

William S. Stavropoulos
Founder and Chairman, Michigan Baseball Foundation

Part I:

A Dream Come True?

CHAPTER *1*
THE CALL.

Hey Terry, Happy New Year." It was December 31st, 2005. The voice sounded familiar, but I wasn't quite sure at first who'd left the message on my cell phone.

"I want to talk minor league baseball with you."

I love baseball. This sounds good. And at this point, I realized who was talking. I can't tell you who it was except to say that it was not Scooter Libby.

"I have an exclusive story I want to give to you."

In the television news business, these words are like gold. This sounds even better.

"It's a pretty darn interesting story about what's going on up there in your area. Give me a call sometime."

Sometime? Sometime came as soon as I could find the tiny redial button on my cell phone.

He answered, and this is the story he told me: a couple of former Dow Chemical executives were about to buy the minor league baseball team in Battle Creek, build a new stadium on some property Dow owned in downtown Midland, move the team there, and have everything up and running in time for opening day 2007—which was then about fifteen months away.

By the time the phone call ended, I was standing there in a stunned silence. Did I just hear what I thought I heard? While my source had a great deal of detail, and lots of confidence in what he was telling me, it was still difficult to believe. But what if it was true? What an incredible story! Could it be possible that it really was an exclusive story, and that I was the only one in the media to know about it? It's a big deal in my business to break a story like the one that was just handed me; it's why reporters go to work each day. We live to report a story like this.

But there was a lot more to it than that. Competitive instinct aside, if the story panned out, it wasn't just good news for me. It was good news for a part of the country that badly needed some good news, a story about something besides plant closings and hard times—a story about something that might make a difference for the better.

Which would *also* be personal good news for me. I live in central Michigan. I love it. I plan to spend the rest of my life here, and I want my children to be able to live here too, and not have to move away to find a job.

And, not so incidentally, I was excited because I'm a baseball fan, and being a baseball fan in Michigan hasn't been all joy and sunlight. I'm not exactly sure when it happened, but sometime between my days in college and my current state of middle-agedness, baseball in Michigan had lost its spirit.   The excitement of the game was missing, kids weren't playing the sport as much I did when I was growing up; they were busy playing soccer and text messaging and updating their MySpace profiles instead.

THE DARK YEARS

You can't really blame them, because for all practical purposes they didn't have a major league team to follow. The Detroit Tigers came back to life in 2006 and are now doing some pretty exciting things, but that comes at the end of a long, long dry spell. Before then, the Tiger had last won a World Series in 1984 and last made the playoffs in 1987. They weren't just bad, they were rotten; they were so bad that in 2003, after beating the Minnesota Twins in the last game of the season, they ran on to the field, jumped into each others arms, and danced like they had something to celebrate. And what, you may be wondering, were the Tigers so excited about? Had they perhaps won a championship? No. What brought all this on was the fact that by beating the Twins they had managed to avoid having their 120th loss of the season.

That was probably the low point, but there had been many bad years before it, and a couple to follow. It was so bad, that at times there were Tigers games available for local broadcast, and some places in Michigan, no station would pay for the rights to show the games. And you know what? I don't think anyone really cared. When I would ask my neighbor's kids who is their favorite baseball team, most would say the Yankees or the Red Sox. When your local big-league team breaks out the Champagne because it only lost 119 out of 162 games, you do not have a situation that's going to cause the kids to drop their Nintendo games and clamor to go to the ballpark. What you have, I thought, looking meditatively at my now-silent cell phone, is baseball apathy.

CHAPTER **2**
WE'VE BEEN HERE BEFORE.

I had to tell someone about this. I called my boss, WJRT-TV News Director Jim Bleicher, and told him about the call I'd gotten. He agreed that it sounded pretty exciting and reminded me that it was New Years Eve, and the Saturday of a three-day weekend. If indeed I had the story as an exclusive, it would keep until Tuesday. If somebody else had it, it would also keep until Tuesday, because nobody would be able to do anything about it until then anyway, including me.

But I wanted to. I wanted to go back to work right that minute. I was thinking, wouldn't it be great? We'll get a minor league team and a new stadium, right here in mid-Michigan, and maybe the Tigers will even have a decent year. Now, I told myself, I'm really dreaming. But the idea of minor league baseball coming to the area isn't so far-fetched. I've been watching it try to come to this part of Michigan for years now. And I want it. We *all* want it.

A WHOLE NEW BALLGAME

First let's talk about minor league baseball, which has changed dramatically in recent decades. The quality of the players hasn't changed—these are still ballplayers waiting for their chance to make it to the big leagues—but just about everything else has. It is, you should pardon the expression, a whole new ballgame, and it's not really about baseball; it's about family entertainment. Some innovative people figured out that if you give fans more than just a baseball game to watch, they will come, and when they come to games, they will shop and eat at surrounding stores and restaurants. A great example of this is in Dayton, Ohio, home of the Dayton Dragons, a Single A affiliate of the Cincinnati Reds in Minor League Baseball's Midwest League. They built a $22.7 million stadium in Dayton in 2000, and every game has been sold out since. The stadium, in fact, has been credited with helping create a rebirth of that rust-belt city.

Why are people showing up at the Dayton games? Oh sure, if you buy a ticket, you can watch nine innings of baseball at Fifth-Third Field, but is that really the draw? No. You really never know how these teams are going to perform on the field; sometimes they're fun to watch, and sometimes you sort of want to avert your eyes.

People turn out for the games anyway. They come out first of all because it's affordable: the highest ticket prices for the nicest seats in the newest stadiums are right around the twelve-dollar range, compared to a hundred dollar tickets at big league stadiums—which means a family of four doesn't have to take out a home equity loan to go to see a professional baseball game up close. They also come out because it's pretty much a guaranteed good time. Baseball's not the only attraction at the games; for example, in Dayton, behind the outfield wall at the ballpark there's an inflatable castle the kids can play in. The children are also invited to dance on top of the dugouts with the team's mascot. If I were to ask my kids if they wanted to go see a minor-league baseball game, they might yawn and say no. If I asked them if they wanted to go play in an inflatable castle, they'd beat me to the mini-van.

Dayton Assistant City Manager Stanley Early says that without question, bringing minor league baseball to Dayton has been an overwhelmingly positive experience for the city. Not only has the stadium and team boosted the local economy, it has helped bring a city together; an urban-suburban split has been blurred by the thousands of fans who come from all across the Dayton region to the downtown area seventy nights of the year. He says it's difficult to come up with any negative impact the project has had over the last seven years.

That's why some city and county leaders have been looking very seriously at attracting a minor league baseball team. It's not about the baseball so much, it's about improving the region's quality of life. A new, fancy stadium can improve a region's image, which means a company thinking about building a new plant or facility might give that area serious consideration when deciding where to build it. They want their workers to have things to do on their off time with their families, or fresh entertainment for single professionals, and what could be better than going to an affordable, clean, fun, family-oriented professional baseball game?

THE RISK FACTOR

Which raises an obvious question: if a minor-league baseball team is so great, why doesn't every town have one? The answer is (a) there are only so many teams to go around, and (b) to make a go of it you have to have a new, modern stadium—and to have that, somebody has to pay for it. Over the years, these two factors have combined in various ways to thwart the coming of minor-league baseball to mid-Michigan.

Not that people haven't tried. Back in 2000, there were some serious conversations about putting a team in Bay City. To understand what that was all about you have to realize there are actually two minor leagues, affiliated and independent. In affiliated minor league baseball, each team is affiliated with a team in Major League Baseball. The major league club will send its younger players to the minor league affiliates, sometimes know as the team's "farm system," to gain experience. These teams fall under the umbrella of the organizations known as Major League Baseball and Minor League Baseball.

Then there are independent league teams, which are not affiliated with Major League Baseball or Minor League Baseball, and whose players do not have major league contracts. Affiliated minor league ball follows Major League Baseball's large territory boundaries and rules, whereas independent league teams can be anywhere; at the start of the 2007 baseball season in Michigan, for instance, there were independent league teams in Traverse City, Kalamazoo, and Battle Creek.

A LEAGUE OF THEIR OWN

Got all that? Okay; enter Tom Dickson and his wife Sherrie Myers, owners of the Lansing Lugnuts. Dickson and Myers come out of advertising and publishing (he was a senior vice-president at Leo Burnett, she held various management roles at the *Chicago Tribune, Sunset, Smithsonian,* and a number of other publications, including some she launched herself). They acquired the team that became the Lugnuts in 1993, and by 1996 had moved it to Lansing, arranged the construction of Oldsmobile Park (which, like Fifty-Third Field in Dayton, has helped revitalize the city's downtown area), and in general have emerged as a great minor league baseball success story. They understand, and have effectively capitalized upon, minor-league baseball as a vehicle for fun family entertainment.

Photo © Professional Sports Marketing Inc.

Tom Dickson and Sherrie Meyers, owners of the Midwest League's Lansing Lugnuts, explored the idea of an independent league in the area. Later, Tom was to play a key role in bringing the Loons to Midland.

So in 2000 they came up with the idea of expanding into the world of independent league baseball by developing an independent league across the Great Lakes region. (The Lugnuts are affiliated—with the Toronto Blue Jays—not independent. This was to be a separate venture.) They had come up with a very aggressive plan to bring minor league baseball to new markets. In Michigan that summer, they spoke with city officials in Bay City, Flint, and Traverse City. Other locations they scouted included North Chicago and Joliet, Illinois; Gary, Indiana; and East Lake, Ohio.

THE BALLPARK FACTOR

For this plan to work, however, each of these cities would have had to build a new stadium. You cannot, today, make money on minor league baseball in an old ballpark; you need luxury suites and entertainment for the kids and—well. You need a new facility, period. Dickson and Myers understood that perfectly, and realized before long that they had bitten off more than even they could chew. It was going to be very difficult—in fact, it was probably going to be impossible—to get every community they targeted to build a new stadium. (I'll tell you a little more about *why* that's so hard in a minute.) Shortly after that visit to Bay City in 2000, Dickson and Myers decided to scuttle their plans for an independent league and concentrate on affiliated minor league baseball.

(And, just to nail the lid down flat, a few years later Major League Baseball and Minor League Baseball began enforcing a standing rule that owners of affiliated minor league teams cannot own an independent league team at the same time.)

WALKING CATFISH?

Our next brush with minor league ball came in 2003, when the owner of a minor league team in the Kansas City area scoped out the tri-cities for several days. Nothing came of that, but the following year a more determined attempt was made to bring minor league baseball to the area by David Heller, owner of the Columbus (Ga.) Catfish. This was precipitated by a chance meeting between his wife, June, and Judy Brunner, wife of Bay City councilman Charles Brunner, at a United Auto Workers conference in Washington. During the course of the conversation, the two women discovered mutual roots in Michigan (June Heller is originally from Grand Blanc) and a mutual interest in minor league baseball.

Heller himself, meanwhile, was exploring the idea of relocating his team from Columbus to another city that might prove less resistant to building a new stadium for it. Apprised by his wife of her conversation with Judy Brunner, he and his business partner, Bob Herrfeldt, made arrangements to give a

David Heller alongside the Saginaw River as he prepares to give his pitch for minor league baseball to Bay City community leaders, July 7th, 2004.

presentation to city commission members and other city and Bay County officials in March of 2004. After the presentation, which reportedly went very well, Heller told reporters he planned to buy a different minor league team and move it to Bay City, leaving the Columbus Catfish in Georgia. (This, it turned out, was not true, as the plan all along was to have the Catfish move to mid-Michigan.)

So far, so good. Bay Area Chamber of Commerce President Mike Seward, who had experience in attracting professional sports teams (he'd helped engineer the relocation of an NBA team to Sacramento, CA) was on board, as were other city and county officials. It was arranged that Heller and Herrfeldt would come to Bay City again and make a presentation to an audience of community and business

27

leaders and the public as part of a special Bay Area Chamber of Commerce Luncheon.

BATTER UP

The luncheon was scheduled for July 7th. When I interviewed Heller that morning, he told me the Bay City area was close to becoming an entertainment and recreation mecca and "a baseball stadium was the fuel to light the rocket."

What Heller presented was a fairly well-developed plan, at least from Heller's and Herrfeldt's perspective, hammered out in conversations with Bay City officials in the months since their first meeting. The idea was that forty-eight acres of prime riverfront property, later known as Uptown at Rivers Edge, would be part of a

Photo © WJRT-TV.

Columbus Catfish owner David Heller speaks to Bay City community leaders at the Doubletree Hotel and Conference Center about bringing a minor league team to mid-Michigan.

development and financing deal for a new stadium. The city would give ten acres free of charge to Heller to build the baseball stadium and sell the other thirty acres. The profit from the sale of that property would go to help pay for construction and infrastructure costs. The city and/or county would have to sell bonds as well, but the property taxes generated by the land would help pay off the debt.

Heller himself would contribute up to ten million dollars to the project. The plan was to build a twenty-million-dollar stadium and a condominium development with one side overlooking the ballpark and the other looking out on the Saginaw River.

The final detail to be ironed out was the fact that the Midwest League at that point had fourteen teams. You can't add just one team to a league, because there needs to be an even number; you have to add two. Heller had that figured out; he would move the Columbus Catfish to Bay City and another minor league team in East Lake Ohio would move into the Midwest League. So everything was set but the land and the money.

POP FLY TO THE INFIELD

Unfortunately, that stalled the deal. Most new baseball stadiums are built at least in part with public funds, i.e., taxpayers help pay for the construction of these facilities. An example is Lansing's Oldmobile Park, which was built for $12 million back in 1996. There are stadiums built with private funds—the Grand Rapids baseball stadium, Fifth Third Ballpark home of the West Michigan Whitecaps, was built in 1996 solely with money raised by the owners of the team and other investors—but it's rare. Heller's plan for Bay City depended on the availability of public funding.

So it was a blow when Bay City Mayor Robert Katt (who has since passed away) came to the podium and said flatly that no taxpayer money would be used to help finance any baseball project. A few days later, city leaders said they wouldn't allow a stadium to be built on the Uptown at Rivers Edge property. They did not want to put a ballpark on prime real estate and take a chance that the team would go elsewhere after five years or be a financial flop, leaving them with a ghost stadium to fill.

Some Bay City community leaders were even skeptical that Heller could pull this whole thing off. While they thought baseball would work, they weren't comfortable with Heller's style. The city refused to sign an exclusivity agreement with him, meaning the community could talk to other people interested in bringing minor league baseball to town.

Finally, it turned out that the Uptown At Rivers Edge site had been established with the assistance of a state grant—on the condition that no baseball stadium or casino would be built there. There were theoretical solutions to most of these problems, but realistically, from that point on, the chances of Heller moving the Columbus team, or any other team, for that matter, to Bay City were pretty much gone.

CHAPTER **3**
TRACKING THE STORY

A nother disappointment—but now, out of the blue a year and a half later, it looked like maybe something was really going to happen. All through the New Years weekend I kept asking myself if this story could really be true. The business about ex-Dow executives buying the Battle Creek team and moving it to Midland seemed plausible enough, but having the team in town *and* a stadium built by opening day 2007? Maybe somebody was pulling my leg. This was New Years, not April Fools Day, but who knew? The pranksters might have been getting an early start.

(Memo to any young reporters who may be reading this: never—never ever ever ever ever—trust a hot tip you get on April 1st. Here's a good example why. On that date in a certain year in the late 1980s, a Michigan radio station (I will not identify anyone in this story to protect the embarrassed, but I will tell you that I had nothing to do with it) ran a report that the Detroit Tigers had been sold to the Sony

Corporation, and that the team was being moved to Japan. Sadaharo Oh, one of the great home run hitters in Japanese baseball history, would replace then-Tigers manager Sparky Anderson. The "breaking news report" included an interview with someone speaking broken English who claimed to be Sadaharo Oh himself. Even though it was April Fools Day, and even though the story was obvious nonsense— as one call to anybody at the Tigers, in fact one call to anybody in Major League Baseball, would have revealed instantly—a TV station treated the story as authentic. A reporter stepped in front of the camera, reported the Tigers were moving to Japan, and said they would have more "as the story developed." Then, red-faced, they went back on the air to apologize and explain that they had been the victims of a practical joke. So if somebody calls on April 1st and tells you the sun is shining, don't run the story until you've gone outside and had a look at the sky.)

THE LONG WEEKEND

New Years Day was a Sunday, which meant Monday was a holiday. Normally I love a chance to spend a little extra time with my family, but that particular Monday was just one more thing between me and what I wanted to do. Finally it was Tuesday, and I could start actually working on the story instead of obsessing about it.

I didn't want to call anyone at Dow Chemical until I had good reason to believe the story was accurate, because I didn't want to tip someone off that I was working on it. If you get too close to the center of the story too early, somebody may say, Oh guess what this reporter asked me? Then they tell somebody else, and the somebody else tells two more people, and before you know it, your "exclusive" is all over town.

Not gonna happen—this was *my* story. I picked up the phone and called Alan Stein, Chief Operating Officer of Ivy Walls Management and principal owner of the Southwest Michigan Devil Rays, the minor league team in Battle Creek. I knew there was *something* going on down there; a few months earlier, in the fall of 2005, the team had started a promotional campaign to increase the number of season ticket holders. The deal was that if they sold about 1,800 season tickets, the owners would build a new stadium in the Battle Creek area, keeping the team in southwest Michigan. (A tall order; the previous season the team had sold only 300 season tickets.) If they didn't hit their season ticket goal, all bets were off. The owners might move the team, or they might sell it.

When you make a call like this, you have to listen very hard to how the person on the other end of the line responds to your questions. It's not exactly what they say, it's how they say it. When I got Alan Stein on the phone, I had a feeling he was expecting my call. To sum up the conversation, he said that they were disappointed with the number of season tickets they'd sold in the promotional campaign, that they were looking at their options, and that he would make a decision within two weeks.

I asked if he was thinking about selling the team to a group of investors from Midland. He said he wouldn't comment on a specific potential buyer, but he did confirm he had talked about selling the team to "certain individuals."

HMMMM . . .

That told me a lot. He could have denied the Midland investor group story, but he didn't. There was something there—maybe. It was a start, but I had a long way to go if I was going to get a story on the air that night.

I find it's much easier to talk to someone in person to get a read on what they know or don't know, so it was time to hit the road and see what else I could find out. My photographer Eric Fletcher and I took off for Midland, which is about 30 minutes from our station. I semi knew what I was looking for: another thing my New Years Eve tipster had said was that there was supposed to be a foundation helping pay for the team and the stadium. Our first stop was the Midland Community Foundation, where I spoke to a very nice woman who, when I asked if she knew anything about the foundation helping buy a minor league baseball team, clearly had no idea what I was talking about. Scratch that; as I walked out of her office, I wondered if *I* knew what I was talking about. Foundation? What foundation?

Eric and I were walking down Main Street in downtown Midland, trying to figure out our next move, when we noticed a newspaper stand. Inside was the Midland Daily News, with this headline:

Dow Chemical had asked the city to rezone these 20 acres—but why? If only trees could talk!

"Dow Eyes Land Zoning Change." I thought, that's interesting. I wonder if they are asking for that zoning change to build, let's see, maybe a baseball stadium? In which case the Daily News already had the story. Rats! But no . . . in the article there was no mention of why Dow Chemical was asking the city to rezone 20 acres of property in downtown Midland. They just were, end of story.

So now we knew our next move; Eric and I hotfooted it to the Midland City Manager's office. Karl Tomion, the City Manager, didn't have time to see me on that impromptu visit, but the assistant city manager, Jon Lynch, did have a few seconds. I asked him about the rezoning request and he said he was not sure why Dow Chemical was asking the city for the change. There could be a number of reasons a company would ask to rezone some of its land, but the question I wanted answered was this: would the rezoning of the property allow for a baseball stadium to be built? After looking at the list of possible uses for such a rezoning request, Lynch said yes. The way current zoning stood, you couldn't build a ballpark there, but you could if it were rezoned the way Dow had asked for it to be rezoned.

I had the interview with Lynch on camera. I had a source telling me a plan was in place where Midland investors were buying a minor league baseball team and build a stadium in Midland. I had the owner of that minor league baseball team not denying the possible sale of the team. I believed I had a story, but first it was time to call someone at Dow Chemical Company.

THE SOUNDS OF SILENCE

It was now about 2:30 pm, which meant I would have to decide soon whether I could get this story on the air. I know several people on a professional basis at Dow, but I also knew that getting this story confirmed would be difficult. Sometimes the best way to get a reaction from someone is to just lay your cards on the table, so that's what I did. I called the Dow contact I thought was most likely to be willing and able to help me, and I said, "I understand that two former Dow Chemical executives are spearheading an effort to buy a minor league baseball team in Battle Creek and move that team to Midland, where a stadium will be built. I understand that a good part of the funding will come from a foundation, and that play will begin in April of 2007. Do you know anything about this?"

On the other end of the line I heard nothing.

Silence.

Then a "hmmm."

More silence.

"Hello?"

I heard paper shuffling.

I looked at my watch. It was now 2:38 pm. I was half an hour from the station, and I had to go on set at four. It was getting to be now-or-never time.

Then finally, my informant at Dow said, "I don't know anything about the Battle Creek team. I'm not sure about the two former executives part. But overall, you are on the right track."

Not the greatest confirmation of a story I have ever received, but for me, at this point, it was close enough. I called my bosses and told them I had the story, and scrambled back to the studio. The story aired during our 5pm news on Tuesday, January 3rd, 2006. I was walking on air.

THAT LONESOME FEELING

For about a day. The next morning, I was sure every other news organization in the area would be out there hunting this Midland baseball story and advancing it even further. That's what I do when I have to follow-up on a story; I try to make it my own.

But something strange happened on that Wednesday, January 4th:

nobody else touched it. The only media outlet that did anything with the story was the Midland Daily News. They quoted my story, and along with it they quoted community leaders saying they didn't know anything about this project. What they were saying, essentially, was that Terry Camp is full of it. He is chasing a wild goose.

It was a scary moment. As I said, it is good to be the first reporter on a story. It is a lot less good to be the *only* reporter on a story. Was I wrong? Had I been set up? Had I done someone a terrible wrong, and this was their revenge? Had somebody concocted a conspiracy to trick me into reporting a false story to sabotage my career? Had I ever attended any type of school with Karl Rove? Where *was* everybody?

At which point I received a cryptic e-mail that said "Don't count your chickens before they're hatched. A lawsuit could be coming out of this situation that might affect the Battle Creek team going to Midland."

Oh great, something else to worry about. *Now* what? This, as it turned out, had to do with an attempt by an attorney in Marion, Illinois to purchase the South Bend team, which would allow the Battle Creek team to move to South Bend—I'll explain later—but right then it made me very nervous. Did I report the story too soon? Could something come up that would kill the whole deal?

The next day I called the person who gave me the original story on New Years Eve and poured out my worries. Fear not, said the source;

I *told* you not many people knew about this, right? I'm sure there's a lot of scrambling going on behind the scenes; meanwhile, you have the story, so why not push it a little further? The source gave me two more details: the architectural firm HOK Sport had been hired to build the stadium, and Tom Dickson, owner of the Lansing Lugnuts, had signed on as a consultant to help pull the whole deal together.

Which, as far as I understood it, made sense. I didn't know beans about HOK Sport, but I knew who Dickson was, and that if there was anybody in Michigan who could coordinate something like this, he was probably the guy. So I was either (a) farther ahead of the competition than ever, or (b) on ice of an increasing thinness.

A VOICE JOINS THE CHORUS

Meanwhile, the website ballparkdigest.com was now reporting the story, with the added detail that the team the Midland investors would buy was the indeed the Southwest Michigan Devil Rays. I hadn't reported the team's name on Tuesday, so wherever ballparkdigest. com got its information, it wasn't from me. Which meant there was another source, which meant there probably *was* a story. This made me feel better: if I was wrong, at least I wasn't wrong alone.

So I played the chips I had. On Wednesday, we ran a story on how HOK Sport had been hired to design a stadium, and on Thursday, we told our audience that Tom Dickson, owner of the Lansing Lugnuts, was involved as a consultant to the Midland investors

Photo © Jeff Glenn Photography.

Jenée Velasquez, Executive Director, Herbert H. and Grace A. Dow Foundation, announces the formation of the Michigan Baseball Foundation, January 12th, 2006.

But at this point it was all still just me and the website guy. On Friday, in fact, another news organization reported they "could not confirm rumors" that a minor league baseball team was coming to Midland. Rumors? I've run three stories on this project, and they're calling it *rumors?* This was not good—but I was in it now, and no going back. I did stories on Monday and Tuesday about the possibility of baseball coming to Midland, even trotting out the name William Stavropoulos as one of the Dow executives that might be spearheading the project. Finally, on Wednesday the 11th, nine days after our first story aired, the Bay City Times reported that a press conference was scheduled the next day to announce that Midland

41

was getting a minor league baseball team. *Yes!* I followed up that afternoon with a "how we got there" story.

That Thursday, January 12th, a who's who of mid-Michigan business and governmental leaders—and yours truly, cameraman, sweaty palms and all—were on hand at the Valley Plaza Resort in Midland to watch William Stavropoulos walk to the podium and say, "The rumors are true. We are working on bringing a minor league baseball team to the area." That morning, the papers were signed selling the Southwest Michigan Devil Rays to the newly formed Michigan Baseball Foundation. Looking back, I should have felt a sense of

Photo © Jeff Glenn Photography.

A dream comes true. Michigan Baseball Foundation Chairman and Founder William Stavropoulos announces that a stadium will be built in downtown Midland.

satisfaction, but all I remember is having a great sense of relief. I was going to be able to keep my job *and* watch a baseball game.

PART II:
A Man with a Plan

CHAPTER **4**

THE LEADER EMERGES

A s you've probably gathered, bringing a minor league baseball team to a town and getting a stadium built is no small undertaking. You need an organization—an army of skilled and willing hands—and you also need a leader. You need one person, either someone in the private sector with a lot of clout or someone in the public sector in a position of authority, who is determined to make it happen. In Midland there was such a person: Bill Stavropoulos. More than power, more than money, it was because of his sheer determination to make it happen that summers in mid-Michigan will now have an added attraction.

Neither Stavropoulos nor his determination and ability to make things happen were exactly unknown quantities in Midland before this, of course. He started his career with Dow Chemical in 1967 as a pharmaceutical chemist and became Chairman and CEO in 1995. He retired as CEO in 2000, by which time he had led Dow through one of the greatest transformations in its history, adapting it to the global economy and making it the world leader in its field. Subsequent to his retirement, Dow Chemical fell into difficulties; at the request of the board of directors, Stavropoulos reassumed the position of CEO in late 2002. For the leadership he provided over the following two years, he is widely credited not only with having saved the company but with guiding it through another major transformation. Dow is now the largest—and, in the estimation of many industry observers— the best-managed chemical company in the world..

So he went into this baseball project with a good deal of local credibility as a make-things-happen kind of a guy, and also somebody who knows from baseball: Stavropoulos grew up in Bridgehampton, New York, out on Long Island. One of his close friends and schoolmates was a young man by the name of Carl Yastrzemski, who went on to a glorious career with the Boston Red Sox and a place in the Hall of Fame. The two played baseball (and other sports) together from Little League through high school; Stavropoulos was a left-handed hitting first baseman.

By 2005, Dow was back on an even keel, and Stavropoulos and the board of directors had found an able successor as CEO in Andrew Liveris. In October of 2005, Stavropoulos retired—again—as CEO of Dow Chemical and turned his thoughts and energies to an idea he'd been harboring for some time: bringing a minor league baseball team to the Midland area.

SOMETHING FOR THE AREA

Some men in his position would do such a thing for the glory of being a team owner, or to make money in a potentially quite lucrative venture. There's nothing wrong with those motivations—professional sports would not exist without them—but that's not why Bill Stavropoulos did this. In fact, as we shall see, he went to some considerable length *not* to become a team owner or to create a profit-making venture. He thoroughly enjoyed it (one is permitted to have fun while doing good), but he really led the effort to bring what is now the Great Lakes Loons to Midland in order, in fact, to help out a community and a company that have given him so much over the years.

The idea was to enhance the quality of life in the mid-Michigan area and give a much needed spark to the region. To do that in the most advantageous way to the public, he planned to set up the team and the stadium project as a non-profit business. Not only would that mean profits from the team and stadium go back into the community, but there would virtually be no chance the franchise would ever leave the area.

He had, as we said, been thinking about this for some time, doing research, talking to friends in investment banking, and in the world of baseball. Now, in a very low-key way, he started discussing the idea with people in the Midland area. He did it—this is typical of Stavropoulos—without putting himself at center stage. He didn't say, "I want to bring a baseball team to Midland." It was more like, "What do you think about this idea," or "Do you think baseball would work here?"

The responses were always positive. For one thing, it was pretty clear to everybody that the area could use a boost. To say the least, the mid-Michigan area economy has been in a state of transition for a few years leading up to 2006. The auto industry, such an integral part of the region's economy for so many decades, was taking hit after hit: General Motors was hurting, Ford was in increasingly iffy shape, the parts suppliers were struggling to stay open, and "globalization" had come to be the dirtiest 13-letter word most people knew.

VESTED INTEREST

Midland isn't just an attractive little city; it's also world headquarters for Dow Chemical, which is, at $46 billion in annual sales, #36 on the Fortune 500. Dow has about 42,000 employees worldwide—more than 6,000 of them in Michigan.

Even though it's right in our back yard, many people in Michigan are unfamiliar with the products the company makes. I got an eye-opening look into the breadth of the product line not too long ago, right after I had an eye-opening look at a hole a bunch of invading mice had made into my house as they ate their way around an air conditioning line. It was big enough for a badger to crawl through and it definitely needed to be plugged—but how?

I called upon my prime source of expertise for fixing any type of problem inside and outside a home—my mom. She recommended that I go to the hardware store and buy a product called Great Stuff; it's a sealant that comes out like a foam and then hardens, blocking any opening. Much to my surprise, I discovered that the product is made by the Dow Chemical Company. (We no longer have a mouse problem, but if I ever have to repair that air conditioning line, I won't be able to pry it from away from the Great Stuff. I'll have to see if Dow makes "Great Stuff Remover.)

Dow Chemical Vice-President Michael Hayes was designated as Dow's liaison to the community.

The company has a long tradition of allegiance to the community, and it also has a real stake in enhancing the quality of life in the

Midland area, both to reward the company's employees and entice the brightest and best scientists to mid-Michigan—and, more importantly, to keep them here. In March of 2005, Stavropoulos, CEO-designate Andrew Liveris, and Dow Corporate Vice Presidents Luciano Respini and Michael Hayes held a meeting on this subject. As the world continued to evolve toward a global economy, it had become increasingly apparent to all these men that Dow needed to step up its efforts on behalf of the region. The smart young professionals coming here from all over the world would want a dynamic, diverse place to live, and if they didn't have it in central Michigan, they would find it elsewhere with some other company.

In addition to diversity, the executives also talked about bringing an attraction to the mid-Michigan area, some new form of entertainment. Stavropoulos and Liveris asked Mike Hayes to take on a new responsibility within the company. They wanted him to serve as Dow's liaison to the community, enabling the company to better focus its effort by having a single contact point.

Over the summer, several possible projects were mentioned. They talked about a building a big zoo that would rival the Detroit Zoo. Or a NASCAR racetrack, which would attract racing fans from across the country. An amusement park was one possibility, a Cedar Point North. Another project would have created a museum park based on chemistry, similar to Greenfield Village and the Henry Ford museum in Dearborn.

Stavropoulos, meanwhile, had his own idea. In the same low-key manner he'd used in all his discussions of the subject, he suggested that they might want to think about baseball. The idea struck a chord with the others, including Andrew Liveris and community leader Alan Ott, both of whom thought it was an excellent idea. Ott's support was essential, as he was a senior and highly influential figure in the area's community of foundation leaders.

THE EXPERT

Bill Stavropoulos had already done plenty of research on minor league baseball. He had a pretty good idea how much money would be needed, how a team operates, the basics any sensible business person masters while considering a new venture. Up to this point, however, he wasn't sure how you actually acquire a minor league team.

On the Internet he came across the website of Professional Sports Marketing, a company owned by Tom Dickson and his wife Sherrie Myers, the same folks who, a few years earlier, had wanted to set up an independent league in the Great Lakes area and bring one of the teams to Bay City. The couple still owned the Lansing Lugnuts, and in 2003 they purchased the Orlando Rays, which they moved into a brand new stadium in Montgomery, Alabama, where they are now known as the Montgomery Biscuits.

It was an impressive operation. Although attendance has fallen off a bit in Lansing since the team started play there in 1996, fans were still coming to Oldsmobile Park, and the Lugnuts remained one of the Midwest League's top franchises. Even more to the point, while PSM owns two teams, the company also consults others on how to acquire and run a team, and can even provide a sports catering service to handle the food and beverage operation at minor league baseball facilities.

Stavropoulos liked what he saw; he tested his reaction in conversations with other people in the business, including Lew Chamberlain, who owns the West Michigan Whitecaps, Michigan's other team in the Midwest League, and Dick Nussbaum, legal counsel for the Midwest League. Everyone he talked to said the same thing: if you wanted to find a minor league team, Tom Dickson was the guy to help you. Perfect; finding a minor league team was what he wanted to do, and help was what he needed to do it. Stavropoulos reached for the phone.

CHAPTER **5**

THE FAST LANE

Professional Sports Marketing has its administrative offices in Evanston, Illinois, just north of Chicago. Tom Dickson was out for a while on Thursday, September 15th, 2005; when he got back to his desk he saw a note reading "Please call William Stavropoulos, Chairman, Dow Chemical Company."

Thinking one of his employees was playing a joke, he set the message aside and went about his business. The Chairman of Dow Chemical. Right. Why not the King of Sweden, while we're at it? Some time later, he looked over at the note again. On the other hand, it *could* be legit. Couldn't hurt to check. He found the Dow website and clicked on "corporate governance." Son of a gun, sure enough; William S. Stavropoulos, Chairman, President, and Chief Executive Officer. Might be a good idea to return his call.

So he did, and Stavropoulos explained that he was interested in bringing a minor league baseball team to Midland and that he needed help.

Dickson, wanting to make sure the man understood the situation he might be getting into, explained that minor league baseball has completely reformed itself since the early 1990s. The days of *Bull Durham,* when it was largely a matter of interest to baseball fanatics and what mattered to the fans were wins and losses, are long gone. Now it's all about one word: fun. Minor league ball has become a family entertainment package at a decent price, and when you walk out of the ballpark, the team management doesn't really care too much whether your team won or lost. What they really want to know is, "Did you have a good time?"

The two men had a lengthy, amiable chat. Up until the end of the conversation, Dickson wasn't really sure whether, as they say out on the used-car lot, he had a tire-kicker or a buyer on his hands. Sports are fun, and there are plenty of people around with money, which means that someone like Dickson has a lot of discussions that don't really go much of anywhere. Some people he talks to about buying a team are looking long term; they want to know something about it because maybe they want to see about getting a team in a few years. Or never: some people like to ask questions about purchasing a team, and then decide to go no further. So there was no particular sense of urgency about any of this until the end of the conversation, when it began to dawn on Tom Dickson just what exactly he was dealing with.

"Well," he said, winding up, "I guess the next step is for you to come down here and look at our operation. I'll explain how we work, and we'll go from there."

"What are you doing tomorrow?"

Tomorrow? Startled, Dickson replied that he wasn't too busy.

"Good," said Stavropoulos. "We'll fly down."

THE FACTS OF LIFE

The next morning, a four-man Dow contingent—Stavropoulos, Mike Hayes, Director of Community Projects Peyman Zand, and Chief Information Officer David Kepler—flew to Chicago to meet Dickson face to face. On the trip down, Peyman Zand continued his reading: he'd bought the three books about minor league baseball to better understand how the business operates. Once the foursome reached Dickson's office, they talked, naturally, about minor league baseball, which gave Zand a chance to use the expertise he had recently acquired from the books he'd been reading.

"Tell me," Dickson said. He named one of the books and said, "Have you been reading that?" Zand said yes, whereupon Dickson said, "I know that book. The person who wrote it doesn't know anything about how the business of minor league baseball works these days."

Then he explained how it does work. Dickson told the group a new stadium was a must for a minor league team to be successful and cited his two teams, the Lansing Lugnuts and the Montgomery Biscuits, as examples. Both teams have fairly new stadiums, and both are successful organizations.

During the course of a series of discussions it became clear that if the Dow group wanted a minor league team affiliated with one of the majors—a farm team—they would have to buy an existing team. There was no chance of getting an expansion team, because there aren't any. Major League Baseball is not expanding, so Minor League Baseball isn't expanding either. What they needed was to find a situation where a struggling team, unable to make it in one city, finds itself having either to move the team or sell it to someone else. Given their geographic location, their best chance would be to buy one of the fourteen existing Midwest League teams.

A DEAL IS DONE

"Are there," Stavropoulos asked, "any teams available now?"

Dickson didn't know, but he believed that of all the teams in the Midwest League, the one in Battle Creek might be the one most likely to be up for sale.

"Okay," Stavropoulos said, "let's give 'em a call."

Dickson tried to call the owners of the team right there on the spot, but wasn't able to get in touch with them. He told the Midland group he would keep his ear to the ground, and they should do the same;

he'd be in touch with them once he knew more about the intentions of the Battle Creek team, or any other team that might be in play.

Stavropoulos, Hayes, Zand, and Kepler headed back to Michigan. The feeling in the group was that the initial talks had gone well. Tom Dickson was the man: he clearly knew what he was talking about, and would be able to help them if anybody could. Not long after the meeting, Dickson sent Stavropoulos a draft formal consulting agreement for Professional Sports Marketing to help the Midland group secure a minor league baseball team.

A day or two after he mailed the agreement, Dickson got a phone call.

"Tom, Bill here. I got the agreement."

"So, how do things look?"

"Done," Stavropoulos replied.

For a little while, things were quiet. It was clear to Dickson that Stavropoulos and his colleagues were serious about the project—and vice versa—but how long all this might take was anybody's guess. It could be months, could even be a few years; the stars had to line up just the right way, and nobody could control when that happened. So it was a surprise when, less than two weeks after the meeting in Chicago, Dickson phoned Stavropoulos with the news that Professional Sports Marketing had identified a team that might be available for Midland.

The team was, as Dickson had thought it might be, the Southwest

Michigan Devil Rays, in Battle Creek. Owner Alan Stein was willing to sell, and had named a price of $6 million. "Fine," Stavropoulos said. "Take it." Dickson conveyed the offer to Stein, and came back to Stavropoulos with a new price: $6.25 million.

Stavropoulos wasn't about to start counter-negotiating, and possibly endangering the agreement, over a price increase of four percent. "Okay," he said. "Close the deal." His discussions with Liveris, Ott, and other community and foundation leaders had made him certain that the necessary financial support for the team and a stadium could be found in Midland. If not, he pointed out to the other executives involved in the situation, they could always turn around and sell the team again: demand far exceeded supply. It was a no-risk decision.

THE MARION FACTOR

Meanwhile, a minor subplot was taking shape. Although it turned out to be no more than a footnote to the process that created the Great Lakes Loons, it's worth recounting briefly as a window into the world of baseball ownership.

The Midwest League has fourteen teams scattered across six states: Michigan, Wisconsin, Illinois, Indiana, Iowa and Ohio. At the same time Stavropoulos and his colleagues were meeting with Tom Dickson, an attorney from Marion, Illinois named John Simmons signed a preliminary agreement to purchase one of those teams, the

Photo © WJRT-TV.

The members of the Michigan Baseball Foundation, January 2006, as they were about to hold their first-ever meeting. Back row (l-r): Arnold Allemang, Dominic Monastiere, Michael Hayes, and Eric Gilbertson. Front row: John Bartos, Bill Stavropoulos, Jenée Velasquez.

South Bend (Indiana) Silver Hawks, and move it to Marion. This, had it happened, would have created an opportunity for the owners of the Devil Rays to pull out of Battle Creek, where they were saddled with an antiquated stadium and plummeting ticket sales, and move the team to South Bend.

Even though Simmons had an agreement to buy the South Bend Silver Hawks, the sale required the approval of the Midwest League. Stavropoulos and Dickson were all but certain he wouldn't get it, because the other owners in the league were not crazy about the idea of having a team in Marion. Right now the farthest south the league travels is Peoria, Illinois; Marion would be an additional five hours south. Each way. By bus. In addition to the geography issues, there were also some in the Midwest League who had a personality conflict with Simmons. There was a feeling that he was "counting his chickens before they were hatched" by announcing plans to build a stadium for a team that he didn't formally own yet.

Meanwhile, Stavropoulos, Dickson, and the lawyers—their number augmented by a baseball-law specialist from California—worked toward an agreement for the sale of the Battle Creek Devil Rays to what would be known as the Michigan Baseball Foundation.

THE SALE BECOMES OFFICIAL

One of the big annual out-of-season events in the baseball world is the Baseball Winter Meetings. People from both Minor League Baseball and Major League Baseball convene in some sunny place in early December to do business and press the flesh. It's like any other industry get-together. There are social events. There are meetings and seminars. There is a trade show, where exhibitors display everything from stadium seats to bats to hats to turf (artificial and genuine). There is, generally, a certain amount of golf.

And there are league meetings. The owners are all in the same place at the same time, so they sit down together and make whatever major business decisions they need to make. This particular year, 2005, the Winter Meetings took place in Dallas; it was here that the

Midwest League would be asked to give its official approval of the sale of the Silver Hawks.

At Dickson's suggestion, the Midland group flew down to be on hand. John Bartos, a trustee of the Charles J. Strosacker Foundation, and Arnold Allemang, who sits on the Dow Chemical Board of Directors, joined Stavropoulos, Hayes and Zand for the occasion.

The meeting started at around 10 in the morning. On hand was John Simmons, who'd come to the meeting to explain why he wanted to purchase the South Bend Silver Hawks and move them to Marion. It went as badly as had been expected; Dickson, as a consultant to the Midland group, recused himself from voting, whereupon the Midwest League denied Simmons's request by a vote of 13-0.

Simmons knew that South Bend owner Alan Levin was having talks about selling the Silver Hawks with another group spearheaded by former Indiana Governor and South Bend Mayor Joseph Kernan. According to Simmons, Midwest League attorney Dick Nussbaum, who is also from South Bend, persuaded the owners to vote against him, clearing the way for Kernan and his group to buy the team, which would have kept the Silver Hawks in South Bend. Simmons felt he'd been sandbagged, and left the meeting in not the best of moods.

At this point, Dickson excused himself from the main meeting and went to join Stavropoulos and the rest of the Midland group for a face-to-face meeting with Alan Stein.

After an hour of talking, Stein and the men from Midland had a verbal agreement: he would sell them the Battle Creek team. The attorneys on both sides still had a lot of work to do before the papers were ready to sign, but the process was well under way, and now the deal was official.

The men flew back to Midland grinning at each other like kids. In mid-September, they had been hoping they would be able to acquire a baseball team for the area in a couple of years. A little over two months later, they had one more or less in hand.

And now it was *really* time to get to work.

CHAPTER **6**
NOW WE NEED A STADIUM

Once a deal was struck for the acquisition of the Southwest Michigan Devil Rays, a couple of major realities had to be dealt with. The first was the fact that there was, at that point, no place to put them: Midland didn't have a stadium. Accordingly, right after the trip to Dallas, Bill Stavropoulos, Arnold Allemang, and John Bartos formed themselves into a Subcommittee To Do Something About That and started talking to people who design ballparks. It's not a crowded field, and they quickly narrowed their list of candidates to two, HOK Sport and HTNB, both headquartered in Kansas City, MO, and both major players in sports venue design. HTNB is currently working on athletic facilities and stadiums at Oregon State, Arizona State, and USC, among many other projects. HOK Sport is active all over the world; the firm has designed stadiums in Sydney, Australia, Nanjing and Hong Kong, China, London (two stadiums) and other places in the UK, the United Arab Emirates, and all over the US.

What Stavropoulos, Bartos, and Allemang wanted to see was minor league baseball stadiums, and their first stop was Montgomery, Alabama, where they visited Montgomery Riverwalk Stadium, home of the Montgomery Biscuits. The stadium, designed by HOK Sport, was relatively new; its opening game was April 16th, 2004.

Next they headed to Charleston, West Virginia to tour Appalachian Power Park, home of the West Virginia Power, also a Single A minor league baseball team. That stadium opened up on April 14th, 2005, and was designed by HNTB. They also visited Oldsmobile Park in Lansing, another HOK Sport project.

THE NEED FOR SPEED

Both HOK and HTNB told the Midland group they felt comfortable they could have a stadium up and ready in time for the opening of the 2008 season. Stavropoulos said no; that wasn't soon enough. Once the sale of the Battle Creek team to Midland was approved by the Midwest League, the Midland Baseball Foundation would be, until they could get the team moved, the new owners of the Devil Rays. The team would almost certainly lose money during the 2006 season; there was nothing Stavropoulos could do about that, but he didn't want to go through the 2007 season the same way. A ballpark needed to be ready for play in Midland for 2007.

That's why HOK Sport got the job. Bartos and Allemang, the two construction experts in the group, had a methodology that would make it possible to complete a stadium in twelve months. HKO Sport was a little dubious—"I'm not sure," Arnold Allemang says, "they entirely believed we knew what we were talking about"—but they were willing to give it a try.

PUT IT DOWNTOWN

Meanwhile, the location of the soon-to-be-constructed ballpark needed to be decided upon. Stavropoulos thought from the beginning that the best location for the stadium would be in or very near downtown Midland—which is where it ended up—but a number of other sites were considered and even favored by some involved in the baseball project.

One possible location was near the Midland Mall. The thinking there was that people would be able to get off of U.S. 10, visit the mall, go to the game, and then head home. There was also talk about building the stadium out of Midland County altogether, maybe somewhere along I-75 between Saginaw and Bay City, or perhaps in the Freeland area near MBS International Airport.

There were other Midland locations discussed as well. There was talk of building a ballpark south of the Tittabawassee River, near the Tridge. The problem there was that it would have been in a floodplain. Another location was just outside of the downtown area, a little farther east of where the stadium sits now.

But Stavropoulos didn't want the stadium "just outside" the downtown area. He wanted it downtown, so much so that he'd even considered the possibility of not going through with the deal if that didn't prove possible. Part of the magic with minor league baseball teams in these modern times is their ability to change the landscape of a city. Not just the physical landscape, but the economic and social landscape as well. The Dayton ballpark, which has had seven years of consecutive sellouts, brings eight thousand people to the downtown area for seventy nights of the year. Lansing's downtown was revitalized by Oldsmobile Park. The downtown area of Memphis, Tennessee is in the midst of a revival, mainly because hundreds of thousands of people each year come downtown to see the Memphis Redbirds play in AutoZone Park.

So the stadium needed to go right there in downtown Midland. As it happened, Dow Chemical had a perfect piece of property downtown, was available at a perfect price: the company is leasing the property to the Michigan Baseball Foundation for one dollar for the next 99 years.

Which was lovely, but it didn't alter the fact that many, many, many *other* dollars would be necessary.

THE FINANCING PACKAGE

When Stavropoulos started floating the idea of bringing a minor league baseball team to Midland, he had three main concerns about getting the project done. The first was coming up with the financing to buy the team and build a stadium. In September he met with the leadership of the major Midland-area foundations , told them about the possibility of a baseball team in the city's future, and asked if they would be willing to pledge money to make it happen. They were enthusiastic about the idea; they asked to see a marketing plan and a business plan, but in general they gave Stavropoulos what he called an

"Oklahoma guarantee." As long as everything was all right—which, knowing him, they were pretty sure it would be— they were on board.

In November, shortly before his trip to Dallas, Stavropoulos went back to the foundations. The agreement with Alan Stein was far enough along at that point to put together a fairly detailed pro forma business plan, and he also gave them a marketing presentation

Photo © Jeff Glenn Photography.

From one Dow Chemical Chairman and CEO to another; Bill Stavropoulos and Andrew Liveris at the April 11, 2006 groundbreaking ceremony.

74

Michigan Baseball Foundation members at the April 11, 2006 groundbreaking ceremony. Left to right: Dow Chemical Director Arnold Allemang; Saginaw Valley State University President Eric Gilbertson; Dow Corning Vice President Abbe Mulders; Dow Chemical Vice President Michael Hayes; former Dow Chairman and CEO William Stavropoulos; Chemical Bank President Dominic Monastiere; Midland Public Services Director Marty McGuire; Dow Foundation Executive Director Jenée Velasquez; Strosacker Foundation Trustee John Bartos.

on what a baseball team can do for an entire region. They were shown how a team and a new stadium had revitalized downtowns in places like Lansing and Dayton and Memphis. Once the foundations saw the true impact of these projects on the communities, they were more than happy to pledge the necessary funds to make it all happen.

MAJOR CONTRIBUTORS

The Dow Chemical Foundation was the leading financial supporter of the baseball project, but by no means the only one. The Herbert H.

and Grace A. Dow Foundation, established in 1935 by Grace Dow, widow of the founder of the Dow Chemical Company, has more than $500 million in assets, in the form of everything from Dow Chemical Company stock to land to cash. The foundation's goal is to use its sizeable wealth to enhance the quality of life across the entire state of Michigan. Its 2005 annual report shows bequests ranging from $1.5 million to the Nature Conservancy, part of a $4.5 million dollar pledge for land preservation in the Upper Peninsula, to $1,500 to help a local township with the construction of a veteran's memorial.

Jenée Velasquez, executive director of the Dow Foundation, says while there had been other ventures pitched to the foundations about bringing sports teams to the area, there was always concern, mainly because the proposals came from outside investors who might leave town in a few years if there was a better offer elsewhere. But this deal was different. It would be locally owned, with the intention of sinking permanent roots right there in Midland.

The total amount needed to bring baseball to Midland was approximately $35 million, $6.25 million for the purchase of the baseball team in Battle Creek and about $28 million to build a state-of-the-art stadium. (The final cost of the stadium, as it turned out. would be $33 million.) The Dow Foundation felt a baseball project would fit neatly into its goal of enhancing the quality of life in the region, and it pledged $7 million—a lot for an organization

One of the brightest smiles at the groundbreaking ceremony belonged to Linda Stavropoulos, wife of Michigan Baseball Foundation Chairman and Founder William Stavropoulos.

that usually has no more than about $11 million in cash on hand at any one time.

The Rollin M. Gerstaker Foundation pledged $5 million. Foundation Vice President and Treasurer Alan Ott says it was the credibility of Stavropoulos, who also sits on the foundation's board of directors, that was the major factor in making the financial commitment. Ott did a little research by talking to his son who lives in Grand Rapids and goes to many West Michigan Whitecap games. His son told him you never have a bad time at the ballpark. Also on the Gerstaker Foundation board is Bill Schuette, who says Stavropoulos talked to him about the project in the summer of 2005.

Schuette thought it was a tremendous idea; when the "Midland 5" returned from Dallas, Schuette said he didn't need to hear more. He was sold on the project.

An initial offer of $500,000 from the Charles J. Strosacker foundation grew to $1 million dollars because of the excitement surrounding the venture. Another participant is the founder of the Michigan Baseball Foundation and his wife; the William and Linda Stavropoulos Foundation has pledged financial support for the project.

DIRECT CORPORATE SUPPORT

Stephanie Burns, Chairman, President and CEO of Dow Corning, came to Dow Chemical's corporate offices for a meeting with Andrew Liveris. (Dow Chemical owns fifty percent of Dow Corning; Corning, Incorporated owns the other fifty percent.) Liveris needed to talk with Burns about another matter, but he first said, "There's something Bill wants to discuss with you."

Stavropoulos told Burns about the baseball project and that he was looking for financial support. Burns, who remembered all the talk in Bay City about its quest for a minor league franchise, was surprised to hear that Midland was planning on getting a baseball team. She was also excited about the project because it was right in line with Dow Corning's identity as a company that supports the communities it has sites in. Instead of pledging money through the Dow Corning Foundation, she arranged for money to help fund the baseball project to come straight from the corporation.

With a five-year financial commitment from the foundations, the Michigan Baseball Foundation was able to borrow the necessary huge amount of up-front money from the Dow Chemical Company and Chemical Bank. What made minor league baseball particularly appealing to its financial supporters was that the project would be a non-profit entity, which meant money generated

Photo © Jeff Glenn Photography.

Stephanie Burns, Chairman, President, and Chief Executive Officer of Dow Corning, speaks at the groundbreaking ceremony. To her left in the front row are Dow Chemical Chairman and CEO Andrew Liveris, Herbert H. and Grace A. Dow Foundation President Ranny Riecker, and Rollin M. Gerstacker Foundation Vice President and Treasurer Alan Ott.

by the team and the stadium would be put back into community projects. That was also attractive to the Midwest League when it approved the sale of the team to the Midland group. The money donated would go to a new foundation, the Michigan Baseball Foundation. There was no assumption of risk by any one individual and no individual would profit from the baseball team.

Mike Seward of the Bay Area Chamber of Commerce, while he was very disappointed that Bay City would not be getting the minor league baseball team, realized the Midland project would benefit the entire area. And in any case, "We lost out," he said, "to the neatest financial package ever put together to bring a professional sports team to a region."

CHAPTER **7**

NO, NO, THIS YEAR

While funding was the number one concern for Bill Stavropoulos in getting the baseball project together, number two was getting everything done in a timely fashion so the team could open the 2007 season in Midland—which meant, above all, getting the stadium built.

Both Tom Dickson and the architects and project managers at HOK Sport thought it would be better to slow down and focus on getting ready for the 2008 season. Stavropoulos knew delay was undesirable, and he did not accept the idea that it was necessary. The process needed to be speeded up, and the designated speeder-uppers were John Bartos and Arnold Allemang.

They were a good choice. When Stavropoulos was running Dow Chemical, Allemang was his worldwide head of manufacturing and engineering, and he took it upon himself to subject the process of

Photo © WJRT-TV.

July, 2006: just three months after the groundbreaking, the stadium begins to take shape.

building a ballpark to the disciplines he'd helped develop in that role. Bartos is a retired contractor who over the years has worked closely with Allemang and Dow, and is familiar with their procedures and approach; his overall responsibility for the stadium project was overseeing relations among the contractors, the architects, and the project managers driving the stadium construction. As soon as the agreement was signed, Allemang and Bartos sat down with the team at HOK Sport and told them how they wanted to do things.

What ensued was a bracing and highly constructive case of culture shock. Here's the way a stadium is normally built: a client—a municipality, a university, whoever it might be—decides to do such a thing, gets it financed, acquires a site, and hires an architectural firm like HOK Sport to bring the stadium into existence. The architects spend about a year designing the stadium, a process that results in a whole library of design documents laying out in meticulous detail each and every physical aspect of the new facility: steelwork, concrete, windows, electrical systems, plumbing, the works.

83

Then (and, normally, only then) the architects release all the documents at once to the contractors and subcontractors who will bid on actually constructing the stadium. In the process of preparing their bids, the contractors may encounter specifications that, in their view, need to be revised. This can be anything: the placement of a window, the size of a crawl space, the angle of a ramp—you name it. Somebody has to make a decision as to whether to widen the crawl space, move the window, or whatever, and through the established chain of communication—subcontractor to contractor to architect to client and back again—a decision is requested, deliberated, made, and communicated. Meanwhile, all activity in the area in which a decision is required comes to a halt.

Once the primary contracts have been let, the primary contractors order the raw materials they'll need. The suppliers tell them how long it will take to actually get them the materials, sometimes accurately, sometimes not. If the materials are delayed, the doing of whatever you were going to do with them is delayed as well.

All of which explains why it normally takes 18 months to two years to build a minor league ballpark. That's not how Allemang and Bartos wanted to do things; they wanted to move much faster than that, and furthermore they knew how. "When we were at our peak of expansion at Dow, in the late 1990s," Allemang says, "we were having to bring a new polyethylene plant on line somewhere in the world about every 18 months, just to keep up with demand. To do that, at any given moment you need to be planning one, building one, and bringing one on line." And to do *that,* he and his colleagues and the contractors they used had learned how to move fast.

GETTING IT DONE

The men assigned the actual task of building a baseball stadium in 12 months were Fred Eddy and John Swantek, both of whom have worked for Dow Chemical since the 1970s. Eddy was chosen as the project manager and Swantek was the procurement leader, in charge of construction

contracts. Eddy also asked Swantek to be the construction manager of the project. It would be the first time the two men worked in these roles together on the same venture in twenty years, and it was, of course, for

Stadium Project Manager Fred Eddy directing traffic at the ballpark construction site, July 2006.

each of them their very first baseball stadium.

They were both highly conversant with global process methodology, the overall approach Dow uses in all its construction projects. Essentially it means you don't do things in the kind of sequence

I've just described; you do them all at the same time. To give just one example, there was a concern about steel. Because of the frantic worldwide pace of construction—most noticeably in China, but in other places as well—there's a huge worldwide demand for structural steel. To make sure they'd have it when they needed it, Swantek had to order it before they had the engineering drawings ready—something normally unheard of in stadium architecture. He ordered the steel in April, saying, essentially, allocate eight hundred tons of steel for delivery in August, and I'll get back to you later and tell you how we want it formed.

RAPID DECISION MAKING

The same procedure was followed with other critical components, such as plate glass. (Also in heavy demand; all those buildings in China have windows.) Another work process that ensured the project would get done on time was rapid decision making, which for the architects was another startling innovation. Allemang, Bartos, and—when their duties permitted—Eddy and Swantek set up regular decision-making meetings involving the architects, the contractors, and the client. Some of the architects had never been in the same room with a contractor; they were used to a distant, leisurely decision-making process. Now all the stakeholders were in the same place at the same time, so decision were made on the spot, eliminating weeks and months of potential delay. The idea is, when

Photo © Michigan Baseball Foundation.

Aerial photo of the Dow Diamond under construction, October 15, 2006; photo taken by Fred Eddy from a plane piloted by John Swantek.

problems surface, handle them immediately. If a piece of steel or a board doesn't fit correctly for some reason, you don't wait until next week to come up with a solution. You handle it right now.

One of the first problems that caught construction crews by surprise was the remnants of old service stations underground that once lined Ellsworth Street. Seven sites were discovered and plenty of soil was contaminated. The Michigan Baseball Foundation had a few options, one of which was to leave the dirt there and continually monitor the groundwater in the area. But a decision was quickly

87

made to take out of the 40,000 yards of dirt and remove it from the area. The problem didn't slow construction at the stadium site, but it was one of a number of hurdles the Michigan Baseball Foundation had to get over to complete the project by April 2007.

Another problem was the weather. Eddy says rain showers, very heavy rain showers made life difficult for construction crews. The torrential rains at times during the summer months caused some delays as crews had to let the ground dry out. It got very cold in October when the playing field was installed and the freezing temperatures made from some slippery conditions in the work zone. Frost that would settle on the partially installed roofs would make it too dangerous for workers to be up on, so they would have to wait for the surface to defrost.

LOCAL LABOR, GLOBAL ABILITY

You'll notice in this description that we're talking about using local labor—in a town of 43,000 people—to build a stadium in half the time a large, experienced, global sports facility architecture firm thought was needed. A key factor in this, according to John Bartos, is the degree to which the Dow culture and methodology is ingrained in the community. "I'd say that's about 80% of it," he says. "It's a small town, but it's a small town with a huge company in it, and the company has a longstanding tradition of building plants in towns where everybody—Dow, local construction contractors, the plants and the community—grows together. Over time you develop a high level of trust. It's non-adversarial; we work with the company, and they work with us, to get the job done in a way that benefits everybody."

Through a series of Dow-sponsored initiatives going back 25 years and more, the Midland-area contracting community has become globally competitive; in terms of cost- and time-efficiency and ability to execute, says Bartos, it is the equal of any group of contractors anywhere. "The capability around here," he says, "took another big step forward starting 15 years ago, when Bill Stavropoulos and Arnold Allemang intensified this 'Dow culture' with what they call the global project methodology. And it shows in the way the stadium construction was carried out. In addition, the commitment and willingness of the entire local community have to be factored in—the other 20% of the equation. Given the time and budget constraints, I seriously doubt this project could have been successfully executed in any other small town in America."

ATTRACTIONS

The stadium will have many attractions, including two outdoor fire pits to keep warm by during those cool spring and early summer nights, as well as two in-stadium fireplaces, one in the lobby and one on the concourse. The concourse can be closed to the weather, so the stadium is useable as a year-round facility. Other features include play and picnic areas for families, and closed circuit TV within the ballpark, and a state-of-the-art scoreboard with three video panels.

It also has solar power. Right from the beginning, the Michigan Baseball Foundation wanted to make a statement with the type of stadium that would be built. The Dow Chemical Company, its subsidiary the Dow Corning Corporation, and Dow Corning subsidiary Hemlock Semiconductor joined forces to make this one of the most-environmentally friendly baseball stadiums in the country.

Just outside the stadium down the right field line are 168 solar panels, donated to the stadium project by Dow Corning and Hemlock (Hemlock makes the polycrystalline silicon that is the main component of the panels, and Dow Corning makes protective coatings for the panels.) The solar panels are expected to produce more than 28 kilowatt-hours of power, enough electricity to power seven homes for a year.

Stadium construction manager John Swantek says that as far as he knows, the Dow Diamond will be the only minor league ballpark that has some type of solar power system. It will produce enough electricity to run the scoreboard for a full season..

Which raises an obvious question: If most of the games are at night, how can the sun power the scoreboard? It doesn't, really. The power it produces during the daylight hours is used to run things like office lighting, refrigeration systems, and computer systems. Excess

A construction site visit, July 17, 2006. Left to right: Mike Hayes, Paul Barbeau, Jenée Velasquez, Abbe Mulders, Fred Eddy, John Swantek, Dow Chemical Controller Bill Weideman, and Eric Gilbertson.

energy produced at any given time will be put on the Consumers Power electrical grid.

The estimated cost of savings for the Michigan Baseball Foundation is $3,000 a year, depending on sunshine. But this is also an educational venture, to inform fans of the capability of renewable energy.

In all, more that sixty different companies helped build the stadium. It most likely won't be completed by the time the first pitch is thrown. Eddy says the parking lots may need one more layer of asphalt, which will be done sometime after the first set of home games. But even if a certain wall isn't painted, or the umpires' dressing room won't have all the electrical work done, one thing is certain; baseball will be played in the stadium on April 13, 2007.

PART III:
If You Build It, Will They Come?

CHAPTER **8**
WHAT'S IN A NAME (I)?

The Tridge Trolls, the Blizzard, and the Skeeters were some of the more than three thousand entries in the Michigan Baseball Foundation's name-the-team contest, which began in March. Like most of the decisions that had been made up to this point, picking a team name was crucial. The name is the launching point for the marketing of the minor league team; it sums up the identity of the franchise, and it's important not to get it wrong.

The MBF had a good example of *how* important it is in the team it had just purchased. Battle Creek got a minor league baseball team in 1995 when the franchise moved to southwest Michigan from Madison, Wisconsin. The first name the owners came up with was the Battle Creek Golden Kazoos, a name that was a big hit with about seven people. Some Battle Creekers didn't appreciate the shout-out to the Kalamazoo area, and most of the rest hated the name either (a) because they just thought it sounded dumb, or (b) because if the name caught on, the fans would start bringing kazoos to the games and blowing on them, an idea which—the kazoo being among the more annoying musical instruments in existence—was too horrible to contemplate. Just to put the cherry on the sundae, there was also a trademark dispute with a local resident, so the name was changed before a pitch was ever thrown. The Golden Kazoos became the Michigan Battle Cats. After switching major league affiliates years later, the name was changed to the Battle Creek Yankees, and then to the Southwest Michigan Devil Rays.

All of which just might have been a factor in the dropoff in attendance in Battle Creek. I was as caught up in the quest for a new name as everybody else, and was thinking about it more like a fan than a reporter until I ran into somebody in Midland who said, essentially, "Hey Camp, you can find out the team is coming, but you can't figure out the name, can ya? We laughed, and I said, "You know, I really haven't tried to find out the name."

I really hadn't, and I wasn't sure what I would do if I found it out anyway. Midland was having a big downtown celebration eight days later, and part of the fun was the unveiling of the team name. I wouldn't want to be a party pooper, would I?

A NICHE FOR THE NOSY

I might, actually. Do you know why people become reporters? You might think we do it because it's a profession that offers a shot—a long shot, but still a shot—at becoming a network anchor and making zillions of dollars. That would be nice, no question about it, but I think the real reason most of us become reporters—and I include my newspaper brothers and sisters in this—is that we're just plain nosy. Our two favorite words are "guess what". We ask questions that are none of our business. We pry. To this day, when I visit my parents (they live in Ubly, in the thumb area of Michigan), I will casually meander over to the counter top where their mail sits, and sift through everything. Why? I just want to know what's there.

There really aren't too many other professions in which you can be nosy and get paid for it, other than maybe becoming a spy. I looked into that actually; after I graduated from Michigan State, I applied for a job with the CIA. I got an interview with a man who called himself Mr. Wilson—no first name, no business card, just Mr. Wilson—in a room at the Ramada Inn near Detroit's Metropolitan Airport. The whole time we talked, he sat in front of an open window with his face in shadow; all I could see was his silhouette. I could tell it was a human being, but other than that, I was clueless as to what this person looked like.

After the interview I took a three part-test. One part was current affairs. I thought I did well on that segment. The next was an essay, in which I was critical of United States policies in the Middle East. This was 1985—different policies—but anyway, I don't think I scored a lot of points there. Third was a psychological test. I answered no to questions like, "Could you live in a country where there are no doctors?" and "Could you live in a country that has a lot of snakes"? I was pretty sure the "no" answers were disqualifying me, even though, when we got to the one that asked if I could kill someone, I got caught up in the moment and answered yes. A willingness to kill, however, apparently didn't outweigh being fussy about doctors and snakes, and they rejected me.

So I became a reporter instead, all of which helps explain why I went looking for the name of Midland's minor league baseball team. I wasn't sure if I would report it, I'm just plain nosy.

I made a few phone calls and found out that the Michigan Baseball Foundation would have to make a trademark request for whatever name they chose. There is a website for the United States Patent and Trademark Office; I queried it to see if the Michigan Baseball Foundation had done that, and got a hit. One word: LOONS. Could that be it? That was too easy.

Michigan Baseball Foundation Communications Director Stacey Trapani (third from left) with Dow Chemical Public Affairs employees (l-r) Jennifer Holzinger, Garrett Geer, Kristi Reddick, Terri Johnson, and Harold Nicoll.

Photo © Jeff Glenn Photography.

This was on a Friday ; the name was to be unveiled a week from Saturday. Just to see if I'd actually found what I was looking for, I called Stacey Trapani, the team's communication director, and asked a question about how things were going "for the LOONS."

"The what?"

"The LOONS."

"That's not the name," Stacey said.

I told her that was okay, it was just a guess. Then I told her what the guess was based on. She didn't confirm it, but I had a feeling I had the right answer. I told her I would not report the name over the weekend, and I would get back to her on Monday.

That Monday morning, Stacey told me that the Michigan Baseball Foundation was split on whether I should report the name of the team. One of the people not in favor of me putting it over the airwaves was Bill Stavropoulos. I told Stacey that if Bill was against it, even if he was the only one against it, we would not broadcast the name. This was a person that has worked too long and hard on this project, and I didn't want to spoil Saturday's big event.

BUT WHAT KIND OF LOONS?

There are two parts to a team name, the geographical name and the nickname: New York Yankees. Boston Red Sox. Lansing Lugnuts. While the fans were asked to submit their suggestions for a nickname, the Michigan Baseball Foundation and other staff decided on the geographical name. Among the finalists were Great Lakes, of course, along with Tri-City, Saginaw Bay, and Mid-Michigan.

It was very important to get this right as well. Right from the beginning, Bill Stavropoulos had stressed that this wasn't Midland's team and it wasn't the tri-cities' team; it was the entire region's team. It was Mount Pleasant's team, Pinconning's team, Clare's team. If you felt you could drive to Midland for the game, it was your team too. The Michigan Baseball Foundation wanted to draw from a large fan base, and a big step in that direction was giving the team a regional name.

So while, Tri-City was a possibility, they felt it didn't cover all the surrounding counties whose fans would come to games. Saginaw Bay was discussed, but again, not a big enough geographic title. And while Mid-Michigan was the odds-on favorite, in a way, its an overused geographic designation. Even Lansing, home of the Lugnuts is considered to be in mid-Michigan, but it really doesn't cover the northern tier counties. (For my own two cents as a broadcaster, I'm actually tired of saying mid-Michigan, we use it so often during newscasts.) So early on in the naming process, Great Lakes emerged as the geographical part of the team's name.

A selection meeting for the nickname was held April 3rd. The final decision on the name of the baseball team was made by a small group, about seven or eight people, one of whom was Tom Dickson, who, along with his wife, had experience at selecting highly marketable nicknames. The name-the-team contest was still going on at this point, but the feeling was that the bulk of the entries were already in. The group would select their favorite name up to this point, and monitor the new entries in case something better came along.

The Michigan Baseball Foundation needed to move ahead, because there was a lot to do after making the selection. Before the new name could be announced to the public, Minor League and Major League Baseball would have to sign off on it, trademark issues would have to be dealt with, a logo would have to be designed, and clothing would have to be manufactured.

The nickname fans submitted most was the Trolls or Tridge Trolls, in honor of the Tridge in Midland, a three bridge structure over the Tittabawassee River. However, there was concern that the name focused too much on the Midland area; another consideration was the fact that residents in the Upper Peninsula refer to people living in the Lower Peninsula as trolls who live "Under da Bridge", as in the Mackinac Bridge. It made several selection cuts and got the most votes, but the nickname Trolls would not be the winner, something it had in common with Al Gore.

Lumbermen got a lot of consideration, in reference to the early lumber days of the Saginaw Valley region. A weather name was also considered for a time, either the Blizzard or Twisters.

The three names that made it to the final vote were Skeeters, Beacons, and Loons. In the final vote, one person voted for Skeeters, while the rest voted for Loons. And with that, the decision was pretty much made;

unless somebody came up with a really spectacular alternative, the name of Midland's minor league baseball team would be the Great Lakes Loons.

The team's new identity.

No one did. Randy Trudell, from Pinconning, and Shawn Zebrak, a student at Adams Elementary in Midland, both submitted the nickname Loons and will each get season tickets for the Loons' first season.

THE NAME IS ANNOUNCED

Saturday August 26th, 2006, was a cloudy day with rain threatening by three in the afternoon in Midland. The downtown celebration had begun; thousands, and I do mean thousands, had gathered behind the Ashman Court Hotel, where a stage was set up, along with a video screen. Believe it or not, I almost missed the event. My photographer and I were to meet at a gas station in Freeland and drive together to Midland for the ceremony. I gave some bad directions to my photographer and I called Stacey to tell her we were running late and to find out if the event was going on as scheduled.

Stacey said, "Yeah, it's going right on schedule and I don't think we can slow it down." I told her I would do the best we could. We got there at 3:03, and the name had not been announced: we'd made it. (About two weeks later I found out the MBF had slowed the event down just a tad to give us time to get there, which was very kind of them; missing the official announcement would have been tough to explain to my bosses.)

The team name was unveiled via a cartoon video, played to the music of Lenny Kravitz's, "I Want To Fly Away." In the video, a loon flies over Midland and into the stadium, an egg cracks, and the name is revealed. Great Lakes Loons!

Once the name was shown on the video screen, there was plenty of applause among the four thousand people who watched the name being unveiled. The Michigan Baseball Foundation had T-shirts and hats already made, and a mock Midland Daily News special edition was being handed out to the fans. The celebration turned downright giddy. But shortly after the ceremony, I could tell that

The name Great Lakes Loons projected on a huge video screen in Midland to eager fans.

noteveryonewaspleased with the selection.

The first person I walked up to had this say: "I hate it."

"Don't sugar-coat it," I said. "Tell me how you really feel."

"All right," he said, "I *really* hate it."

He wasn't alone. The Midland Daily News started an online poll to get people's reaction. I can't remember the exact numbers from the first day days of voting,

An estimated 4,000 people turned out for a Midland celebration on August 26, 2006, where the name of the new baseball team was revealed.

but if my memory is correct, I believe a whole bunch of people hated the name, and a small group of fans loved it. I even got an e-mail from one person who asked me to do what I could to get the named changed.

This wasn't the first time initial public reaction to a team's name had been unenthusiastic. The Golden Kazoos were an extreme case, but when the name of the Lansing Lugnuts was announced in 1996, initial opinion polls gave it single-digit approval ratings; the same thing happened with the Montgomery Biscuits. Slowly, the locals were won over, and now the Biscuits and Lugnuts rank in the top five in minor-league baseball merchandise sales nearly every year.

THE LOON HUNT

I decided to throw the awesome weight of the media—well, okay, me—behind the new name by putting a loon on camera. I figured I that if I could show our viewers what a cute little water fowl a loon is, it might win them over.

To put a loon on camera, of course, you first have to find one. I was getting reports of loons here and there in the Upper Peninsula, but that was no good; I needed a *local* loon for the audience to rally behind. A little research disclosed the existence of a Loon Lake in Clare County, about forty miles northwest of Midland, and so photographer Brad Jenks and I set out on a loon hunt.

Which turned out to be more adventuresome than we'd bargained for. We knew the lake was in a rural part of the county, but we were a little surprised at just how rural this was; it didn't look like anybody had been on those roads in years. Eventually, we got to where we thought we were supposed to be. We drove through an open gate and into some more ruralness until we encountered a woman who was motoring around on a lawn tractor. We asked her if this was Loon Lake and she said yes, but it was private property; she was the caretaker. I told her why we were there, and she said there were two loons on the lake and offered to help us find them.

Or anyway to look for them. After a half hour of fruitless searching I took out my cell phone and was about to make the call all television reporters hate to make—the one where we have to tell our assignment editor we won't have a story for them today—when suddenly the caretaker said, "That's them! There they are." We drove around the lake to get a better look, and sure enough, there they were.

Photo © WJRT-TV.

A loon on Loon Lake, Clare County, Michigan.

According to the Michigan Loon Preservation Association, the loon is a threatened species in Michigan, with only somewhere around 500 mating pairs on the state's 660 plus inland lakes.

The Michigan Loonwatch program, which keeps tabs on these creatures, is led by Joanne Williams, who lives in Shepherd, Michigan, near Mt. Pleasant. She says the number of loons in the state continues to decline, and that it was a courageous move by the Michigan Baseball Foundation to select the loons as the nickname of the team. She hopes this will bring more attention to the plight of loons in the state. We hope so too.

Who would have thought this would happen? Here we have a

project—a baseball team—started in part by the Dow Chemical Company, a frequent target of environmentalists. The team's nickname was, at least in the beginning, unpopular and somewhat controversial. And who has emerged as perhaps the staunchest supporter of that nickname? An environmental group dedicated to the protection of endangered waterfowl.

CHAPTER **9**
DIVORCED BY THE DEVIL RAYS

*O*nce the team name was revealed, the Michigan Baseball Foundation had only one more secret to keep from me. What major league team will take the Loons as their affiliate? All 30 Major League Baseball teams have young players that they need to develop. They develop those young players in the minor league system, in which each team has a number of affiliates across the country. (We have to explain that concept here in Michigan, because before the year 2006, we weren't sure the Detroit Tigers *had* a minor league system. We had no idea where they were getting those players, and we didn't want to know.)

The Great Lakes Loons play in the Midwest League, which is made up of teams classified as Single A, one of the lower rungs of the minor leagues. (Triple A teams would be one step from the majors, Double A would be two steps; then, in descending order, come Single A, Short Season, and Rookie League.)

Now just because the Loons are a few levels below the majors doesn't mean there won't be quality players in Midland; some pretty interesting people pop up in Single A ball. For example, in 2006 the Detroit Tigers' top rookie pitcher, Andrew Miller, was sent to Grand Rapids to play for the West Michigan Whitecaps, the Tigers' Single A affiliate in the Midwest League. He pitched there about three times before being called up to the Tigers. When Roger Clemens made a comeback in 2006 following his 36th retirement announcement, the Astros sent him to their Single A affiliate in Lexington, Kentucky, to get in pitching shape before returning to Houston. So keep an eye on the roster for these games; you never know who might be out there.

GIVE ME AN AFFILIATE, OR GIVE ME AN ELEPHANT

When Bill Stavropoulos and the Midland group began pursuing minor league baseball, they were determined to have a minor league team that was affiliated with the majors. If they couldn't get that, they would start scouting for giraffes and elephants. (Remember, the idea for a zoo?)

When the Michigan Baseball Foundation bought them in January of 2006, the Southwest Michigan Devil Rays were affiliated with the Tampa Bay Devil Rays. An affiliation agreement, which is formally known as a Player Development Contract (PDC), usually lasts two years. The agreement between Tampa Bay and Battle Creek (now Midland) was due to expire on September 15th. If a major league team doesn't renew its PDC with a minor league team by that date, those teams begin a two-week courting process with other teams that don't have PDCs.

Early on in this whole process, I discovered there was little chance the Tampa Bay Devil Rays would renew their affiliation agreement with the franchise now known as the Great Lakes Loons, because the Devil Rays seem to be moving toward having all their affiliates in the Southeast. Nobody from the Michigan Baseball Foundation actually said so to me, but I don't think they were heartbroken by this development. The Devil Rays . . . how shall I put this? Back in the grimmest of the bad days in Detroit, when the Tigers were losing most of their games and generally dwelling in darkness and despair, they could still cheer themselves up by saying, "At least we're not Tampa Bay."

In any case they didn't renew, so as of September 16th, the Loons had no PDC. Major league teams at that point who didn't have PDCs and were open for negotiations included the New York Mets, the Texas Rangers, the Milwaukee Brewers, and the Los Angeles Dodgers.

The Michigan Baseball Foundation's two picks from this crowd were the Rangers and the Dodgers, and early speculation favored the Rangers. The Loons General Manager, Paul Barbeau, was hired away from the Spokane Indians, a Short Season affiliate of the Texas Rangers. (Hiring Barbeau, incidentally, was one of the early decisions the Midland Baseball Foundation made once it had acquired a team, in December of 2005. "We were all part-timers," Stavropoulos says, "And we needed not only a good general manager but someone who could build an organization. We interviewed several candidates, but Paul was a perfect fit.")

Barbeau has a great relationship with the Rangers, and many inside minor league baseball assumed the Rangers would be the major league team affiliated with the Loons. But something funny happened on the way to Dallas.

SECRECY, SORT OF

I must explain this before I go any farther. Evidently there is some rule which states that the major league and minor league teams involved in this two-week courtship are not allowed to discuss the negotiations—especially not with the media. Now the new kids on the block, the Michigan Baseball Foundation, played by the rules; they told me nothing about who they were talking to about a PDC. However, I was able to get some information from other people in baseball by asking tough, subtle, hard-hitting, probing questions like, "So—who are you talking to? Are you talking to the Loons? How do you think this will all shake out?" People answered freely and at length, making me realize that the gag order on this process was not exactly ironclad.

One of my less-than-clandestine sources was Terry Collins, former Midland, Michigan resident, former major league manager, and at that time, the player development director for the Los Angeles Dodgers. When I called Collins on his cell phone on September 20th, he told me that he would love to have the Dodgers and the Loons come to an agreement, and that he would do everything in his power to see that

Photo © WJRT-TV.

Midland native and former major league manager Terry Collins helped seal the affiliation between the Los Angeles Dodgers and the Great Lakes Loons.

it happened. That night, I aired a story that the Dodgers were in a good position to get the Loons' affiliation, because the guy that was basically calling the shots for that organization wanted to see it happen.

So, as it turned out, did the Michigan Baseball Foundation. Let's face it, the Texas Rangers are a nice organization, but we're talking about the Dodgers here: Jackie Robinson, Sandy Koufax,

Kirk Gibson's World Series home run, all of Steve Garvey's children. What a coup for the Loons to get an agreement with one of the most revered names in all of sports.

The following weekend, Barbeau, Mike Hayes, and Bill Stavropoulos made the decision to take the Dodgers over the Rangers. I got the call Sunday night from a minor league baseball official that the deal was done. Since I already had a story lined up for Monday, I waited until Tuesday before running with it. On Thursday, the Michigan Baseball Foundation held a press conference at Fashion Square Mall with Dodgers' Hall of Fame Manager Tommy Lasorda and Collins. It was another coup for the Loons to get someone with the baseball stature of Lasorda to come to mid-Michigan while the Dodgers were still in the midst of a pennant race. Lasorda, an advisor to Dodgers owner Frank McCourt, was getting plenty of national airtime as Fox Sports was using him in those funny promotional spots for the baseball playoffs, which usually ended with Lasorda giving pep talks to baseball fans whose teams were out of the playoffs by saying "everyone to the t-v."

HEADING EAST

At the press conference, Collins told me that he didn't know how long he would be with the Dodgers organization. He really wanted to get back on the field and be a manager again. Just a week later, Collins took a job as a manager of a team in Japan.

Yeah, I know. Japan? This little development plays a role in our story, which I'll get back to in a minute. First of all, let's talk about managers. Pop quiz:

Who is the manager of the West Michigan Whitecaps for the 2007 season? Former Tiger third baseman Tom Brookens.

Who is the manager of the Peoria Chiefs? Former Chicago Cubs Hall-of-Famer Ryne Sandburg.

The point here is that while there is a chance you have never heard of many of the players in minor league baseball, more and more, the managers are people with marquee names, which becomes an added attraction for the marketing of the teams. Let's face it, who wouldn't want to see the ol' Pennsylvania Poker strutting around in the dugout? Plus, when their team is batting, the manager is the third base coach as well.

The manager for the final season of the

Photo by Patti Tuma, courtesy Michigan Baseball Foundation.

Great Lakes Loon mascot Lou E. Loon and Hall of Fame manager Tom Lasorda at Fashion Square Mall as the Dodgers-Loons affiliation agreement is announced.

Southwest Michigan Devil Rays was former Detroit Tiger Skeeter Barnes. Since the affiliation agreement between the Tampa Bay Devil Rays and the Great Lakes Loons no longer exists, there was no chance he would be heading to Midland. So who would be the first skipper in Loons history?

GOLDEN RESUME

As soon as the Dodgers-Loons affiliation agreement was signed, all eyes turned to Lance Parrish. The former catcher was an eight-time All-Star, won three gold gloves,and played most of his 19 years in baseball in Detroit. Even though he had a great career with the Tigers, it might be easy for some to overlook Parrish's accomplishments. During the 1980s, the Tigers were loaded with stars and quirky characters like Jack Morris, Alan Trammell, Lou Whitaker, and Kirk Gibson. Twenty years later, you might even forget Parrish was on the team because of his quiet, non-controversial demeanor. Many people remember that Gibson hit two home runs in the fifth game of the 1984 series, but many might overlook that Parrish also hit a huge home run in that game as well. During his stay in Detroit, Parrish was one of the more well-respected and well-liked sports figures in the city--and I'm not saying that just because it's possible he might read this book.

Since his playing days, Parrish has stayed in baseball in a coaching capacity, serving as the Tigers bullpen and third base coach, and

Bill Stavropoulos, Paul Barbeau, Tommy Lasorda, and Terry Collins announce the Dodgers-Loons affiliation agreement, September 27, 2006 in Saginaw Township.

Photo by Patti Tuma, courtesy Michigan Baseball Foundation.

even tried his hand at broadcasting. Last year, Parrish was the manager of the Dodgers' Rookie League team in Ogden, Utah, the Ogden Raptors. A logical promotion for him would be to move up to Single A ball and manage the Loons.

As I mentioned earlier, just a short time after the Dodgers-Loon affiliation deal was announced, Terry Collins left his position as the Dodgers director to become the manager of a team in Japan. (See how all this fits together?) Collins, being from Midland, had planned to give the Loons job to Parrish—if he, Collins, had stayed on with his role with the Dodgers. When he left, no announcement had been made about the managerial position in Midland, so things were still up in the air a bit.

The Dodgers hired De Jon Watson to replace Collins. Watson had been the Director of Professional Scouting with the Cleveland Indians for the past three seasons. I gave him about fifteen days to settle into the job before I called him. I asked if he had made any decision on who would be the Loons' first manager. He said, "Oh, I don't want to leak that yet," but by the end of the conversation, I realized he too was leaning toward putting Parrish in Midland. (Watson makes the call as to who will manage the Dodgers' five other minor league affiliates. He'd attempted to get former Dodger and Tiger Kirk Gibson to manage the Las Vegas 51's, the Dodgers Triple A affiliate, but Gibson decided to become the bench coach for the Arizona Diamondbacks.) Watson told me he would probably make the decision sometime before the Winter Baseball Meetings the first week of December. I didn't know if I could wait that long.

COUSIN, COUSINE

The media day for the latest update on construction at the Dow Diamond was November 14th, and following that report on WJRT-TV 12 News, I reported that Lance Parrish was a strong possibility to be chosen as the Loons manager. A couple of other news outlets picked up the story as well, so the next step was to get the official word.

I was sitting in our Saginaw Bureau office one morning with my fellow reporter, Jennifer Borrasso. Jen asked me what I was working on, and I told her I was trying to figure out how I would get it confirmed that Lance Parrish would be the Loons manager. Without missing a beat as she walked by my desk, she said, "Oh yeah, Lance. He's my cousin."

It took a few seconds for it to sink, during which I stared dumbly at her. Then I said, "WHAT?"

Photo © Dave Hinkeldey.

Great Lakes Loons General Manager Paul Barbeau and manager Lance Parrish in Bay City, January 23, 2007.

"Lance Parrish is my cousin. Well actually, my uncle is Tom Parrish and he is cousins with Lance. Doesn't that make me a cousin as well?

I'm not a family tree expert, but that was close enough for me. I asked Jen if she could get Lance's cell phone number, and sure enough, she did. I called the number as I was driving down to Flint on Friday, November 17th and on the other end of line, it was Lance Parrish. After discussing his relationship with Jennifer (Lance thought they were cousins, too) I asked the big question.

"Lance, everyone wants to know up here if you are going to be the manager of the Great Lakes Loons. Are you?"

"Yes," said Lance, "I am."

CHAPTER *10*
WHAT'S IN A NAME (II)?

Sports facilities have been named ever since sports facilities have been built, but it's only during the past few decades that the naming of sports venues, like baseball stadiums, has taken an interesting and expensive turn. Corporations are more than willing to pay millions of dollars to have their name on a place where thousands of people visit, with many more sitting at home, watching the events on television. In a more controversial move, even high schools are being named these days after companies who are willing to pay.

Comerica Bank agreed to pay the city of Detroit and the Detroit Tigers $66 million over thirty years for the naming rights to Motown's baseball stadium, which opened in 2000. (For the first few years of that deal, the executives at Comerica Incorporated can't have been very happy that their name was associated with a ballpark where such bad baseball was being played, at least by the home team. But in 2005, with the All-Star game being held there, and with the resurgence of the Detroit Tigers in 2006, Comerica's leaders must now feel it's money well spent. We'll see how they feel next year.).

The Ford Motor Company is paying $40 million over 20 years for the naming rights to Ford Field, the domed home of the Detroit Lions. (The automaker is paying the money to the city of Detroit and the owners of the Detroit Lions. The Ford family—same Fords—also own the Lions, so how these checks are written, I have no idea. All I know is that if Henry Ford were alive today, he would have these two words to say: "Fire Millen.")

THE NATURAL

When the naming rights issue came up for the new baseball stadium in Midland, it was assumed by many that the Dow Chemical Company would pay to have its name on the ballpark. After all, the stadium sits on Dow Chemical's property. Dow Chemical is paying for the naming rights to the Dow Event Center in Saginaw, home of the Ontario Hockey League's Saginaw Spirit and the host of other activities and shows.

(That facility, incidentally, almost had a different name. In 2001, Saginaw County passed a millage to pay for renovations of what was then called the Saginaw Civic Center. The county was also looking at other ways to raise money, one of which was to have a company pay for the naming rights to the building. Meijer, the discount retail and grocery chain, was one of three companies to get in serious negotiations with the county for the naming rights to the facility, and it almost became the Meijer Event Center. Then September 11th, 2001 happened, and everything was put on hold. When Saginaw County began to talk about the naming rights for the building again, the Dow Chemical Company came forward and won the rights. In 2004, Dow agreed to pay the county and the Saginaw Spirit $2.5 million over ten years for the naming rights to the Dow Event Center.)

When Dow Chemical announced it had purchased the naming rights to the stadium, they asked their employees to submit ideas. The company collected suggestions through the summer months and planned to announce the winning name at a company picnic on October 2nd.

THE SPY

Meanwhile, I found out the name in August. I did it by using the same, hard-hitting, tough-question-asking, investigative reporting I used to find out the team name: I got on the Internet and did a search on the United States Patent and Trademark website. Sure enough, it showed that Dow Chemical had applied for a trademark of the name "Dow Diamond" for entertainment purposes.

I called Dow Chemical External Communications Manager Jennifer Heronema to see if they would be upset if I released the name a little early, and her response was something like, "YES, WE WOULD BE UPSET!" Talk about good at her job; I could hear her actually speak

Photo © Jeff Glenn Photography.

At the company event where the name of the stadium was announced, Dow Chemical's Mike Hayes runs to first base during a baseball game.

in capital letters. I decided maybe I'd just hold off on that story. In any case, the company had been using a diamond-shaped logo since Herbert Henry Dow came up with it in 1918, so I think a lot of people suspected that might turn out to be the name of the ballpark.

On October 2nd, on a cloudy but pleasant Monday afternoon, hundreds of Dow Chemical employees gathered at the picnic, and at the same time, the media gathered to hear the official announcement. Dow Chemical CEO Andrew Liveris was to announce the name after giving a few remarks about the company and the baseball project. Heronema, Brian Wood of WNEM-TV 5, and myself at WJRT-TV 12 News put together an impromptu plan of having Liveris announce the name at about five after twelve, live on our respective noon newscasts.

Photo © WJRT-TV.

On October 2, 2006, Dow Chemical Chairman and CEO Andrew Liveris calls for the name of the new stadium to be unveiled.

Everything didn't go according to the plan.

Andrew Liveris took the stage at about four after twelve, allowing us enough time for the anchor teams in the studio to pitch it to us live in the field, where Brian and I, on our respective channels, would introduce the story and then go to Liveris live to hear the announcement. But he went longer than we originally thought he would, and after at least two minutes, I got nervous. I looked at photographer Eric Fletcher and we both had this look as if to say, "We're in big trouble." This was most likely screwing up the timing of the newscast, which is produced in a way where everything, including commercial breaks, is set to run at an exact time. I was probably given two minutes total for this story, and we were already past that. With a little nod to Eric, I jumped in front of the camera and explained that Mr. Liveris would announce the name shortly, but we would have to get back to the studio. But I added, "By the way, the name of the stadium is the Dow Diamond. Now back to you."

A minute or so later, Andrew Liveris called for a banner which was behind him to be unveiled. At first, the cover the banner didn't unfurl, and with the first recorded save in Great Lakes Loon history, Lou E. Loon, the team's mascot, pulled down the rest of the cover. The name was unveiled.

For $2.8 million over the next ten years, Midland's state-of-the-art baseball stadium will be known as the Dow Diamond.

CHAPTER *11*
A REQUIEM
IN BATTLE CREEK

While Midland and the rest of mid-Michigan were champing at the bit for the next baseball season to start, the baseball fans of Battle Creek were watching the clock run out on affiliated minor league ball in the Cereal City. You're probably thinking well, they couldn't have been too heartbroken over this or they would have supported the team a little better., and it's true: in terms of home-game attendance, the Southwest Michigan Devils Rays were near the bottom of the Midwest League. But it was a hard parting nonetheless, and there are some diehard baseball fans that will always remember August 31st, 2006 at C.O. Stadium in Battle Creek.

First, I must describe C.O Stadium to give you an idea why this version of minor league baseball may not have succeeded in Battle Creek. You know Tiger Stadium? Even though it's a treasure to many people, there are a lot of bad seats in that ballpark. Obstructed view seats, where your vision of the playing field is partially blocked by a huge steel pole, so when you['re watching a double play it looks like the ball vanishes behind the post and then pops out again on its way to first base. Something is happening out there, but you have no idea what. C.O. Brown Stadium has the same problem; huge steel posts obstruct the view of at least half of the fans in the ballpark. Which means it's not fun, and in minor league baseball, not fun equals dead.

THE LAST DOUBLEHEADER

The day before the final game, a water-logged field forced a postponement between the Devil Rays and Beloit, so that final night of baseball in Battle Creek, was a doubleheader. It began at 5:30, with each of the two games being only seven innings long. (Thank goodness for that minor league rule on doubleheaders.)

The first game started with a crowd of seven on hand. I'm not kidding: seven fans, I counted them twice. It was quiet in there, so

Photo © WJRT-TV.

Fans watching the last innings of the last game of the Southwest Michigan Devil Rays, Battle Creek, August 31, 2006.

quiet that from where I was sitting, by the third-base dugout, I was able to carry on a perfectly audible conversation with a lady sitting behind home plate. Man oh man oh man, I thought, these people don't *deserve* to have a baseball team.

But slowly the stadium began to fill up, and when the crowd arrived, they actually saw a pretty good ballgame, albeit one with a weird twist. For the first time in 34 years of Midwest League ball, a pitcher threw a no-hitter, and lost. (Really; Wade Davis of the Devil Rays has the unique distinction of throwing a no-no and still losing one to nothing to Beloit. The baseball gods, clearly, were not smiling on Battle Creek.)

During the break between the first and second game, things got a little emotional. All the fans who had purchased season tickets for the Battle Cats, Yankees, and Devil Rays, were invited to throw ceremonial first pitches for the second game. It was quite a sight. You could tell some of the fans had been practicing for awhile, others you could tell hadn't thrown a baseball in years. One fan even hit a photographer. But as I watched some of these season ticket holders throw, I could see that some of them were shedding tears.

FULL HOUSE

When I looked up in the stands, I could barely believe my eyes. The place was almost packed. My photographer Mike Sanford and I went to get something to eat, and the concessions stands were backed up.

Even the Devil Rays General Manager, Marty Cordero, was taking orders. The gift shop was so packed you couldn't even get inside to see what they were selling. This, I thought, is what it was supposed to be like in Battle Creek for these past fourteen years, but wasn't. And now it was too late.

As the second game moved into the later innings, I talked with several of the fans who'd been season ticket holders for the past fourteen years. Some were near tears, other had been crying off and on during the evening. To them, this was not just a baseball team to come watch on a summer's night. It was a part of their life. One fan was in a wheelchair and needed an oxygen tank to breathe; he told me he wasn't sure what he would do next summer.

(He'll go to a ball game. Battle Creek wasn't without minor league baseball for long; an independent league team in the Northwoods League will be playing at C.O. Stadium in the spring of 2007.)

The Devil Rays looked like they were going to get swept in their final two home games in Battle Creek. They'd lost the first one (the heartbreaker with Davis's fruitless no-hitter) and in the second game trailed Beloit two to one in the bottom of the sixth. (Remember, because of the previous night's rain-out, these games were only seven inning long.)

Then a funny thing happened. Maybe it was those long-time fans yelling for one last rally, and maybe the Devil Rays players heard them, or maybe Beloit was just starting to feel sorry for them, but finally, there was a rally. The Devil Rays tied the game, and then Jackson Brennan (great baseball name) hit a three-run homer, putting the Devil Rays up five to two. Five thousand plus fans went crazy. I got swept up in the emotion of it myself, hugging people I didn't even know.

The final out for the Devil Rays' franchise in Battle Creek ended with a strikeout and a win. As we walked out of the stadium, fireworks went off. As I walked to my car I kept thinking about what one long-time Devil Rays fan told me at the end of the game. She said, "Tell the people of Midland to enjoy this team, and support them. Because otherwise one day the same thing might happen to you—and they'll be gone."

HERE TO STAY

Fan support, of course, was always the one unanswerable question. The team had been found and bought quickly, the financing was brilliantly handled, and the stadium, thanks to the marriage of Dow expertise and the uncanny skill of the local contracting community, seemed to practically spring from the earth. Still, you had to have the support of the people to make minor league baseball take root in Midland. The community leaders wanted it, the Michigan Baseball Foundation wanted it, Bill Stavropoulos wanted it, the leadership at Dow wanted it, and God knows I wanted it. But the residents of the area, the ones who, we all hoped and prayed, would soon be devoted

Photo © Jeff Glenn Photography.

Bill Stavropoulos greeting fans as they stand in line to buy season tickets for the Great Lakes Loons on the first day of sales, August 18, 2006.

Loons fans—how badly did *they* want it?

We got a resounding answer to that question the day the Michigan Baseball Foundation started selling tickets for the coming season. Tickets went on sale at eight a.m. on a cloudy, muggy morning in August at four locations in mid-Michigan, including the foundation's main office on Main Street in downtown Midland. The first ticket-buyer in franchise history, Leslie Watrous of Midland, wanting to make sure she got a good seat, showed up at two o'clock in the morning, and others were not far behind, standing in line for the right to give up their hard-earned cash for a piece of paper certifying they'd bought tickets to sit in a stadium that wasn't even built yet, to watch games that hadn't even been scheduled, to be played by a team that had no name.

By the time sales actually started, a huge line had formed behind Leslie Watrous; among those waiting to buy tickets were Michigan Baseball Foundation member Mike Hayes and Linda

Stavropoulos, the wife of MBF Chairman Bill Stavropoulos, who was greeting as many fans as he could that morning. If the management of the baseball team had any doubts over whether minor league baseball would sell, those doubts ended that morning. Fifty thousand tickets were sold that first day—nearly a quarter of the tickets that would be available for the entire upcoming season. Before they'd so much as put on a uniform, the Great Lakes Loons had swept central Michigan.

Photo © Jeff Glenn Photography.

Leslie Watrous of Midland was on line at 2:30 am on August 18, and became the first person ever to buy a Loons season ticket package.

PART IV:
Root, Root, Root for the Home Team

CHAPTER *12*
WHAT IT MEANS
TO US

Before the Loons came to town, mid-Michigan was the second-largest television market in the country without a professional baseball team. (Orlando's the largest, but in Orlando, during spring training you've got the Atlanta Braves right there at Walt Disney World, plus a half dozen other major league teams an easy drive away.) There are about 82,000 people living in Midland County, about 43,000 in the city itself, and the entire region that the Loons will draw from has a population of more than 400,000.

A report put together in Bay City a few years ago—and carefully studied by the members of the Michigan Baseball Foundation—gives us a pretty good idea of the economic impact the Loons are going to have on this area. The Dow Diamond itself will generate more than $5 million in new revenue each year. That includes ticket sales to baseball games, to high school and college events, and to concerts, premium seating (suites), food and beverage sales, merchandise, naming rights, and broadcasting rights.

People drawn by the team and the stadium to the downtown area will spend another $3 million at hotels, restaurants and retail shops. More than 300 jobs will be created, resulting in more than $12 million in additional gross annual earnings. In total, according to the Bay City report, having a Single A minor league baseball team in the area will inject more than $33 million a year into the local economy

PROFIT POTENTIAL

Not only can it be a boon for the local economy, groups and individuals who own these teams are finding you can make some money with them. Andy Applebee of General Sports and Entertainment, the group that just sold the Fort Wayne Wizards, says "pound for pound, minor league baseball is one of the better values in all of sports." The reason the group sold the Wizards is because they "took it as high as we could," Applebee says. He adds that General Sports is actively seeking other minor league franchises.

John Simmons, the attorney from Marion, Illinois who lost out on his bid to buy the South Bend team, ended up with an independent league team; the Southern Illinois Miners begin play in late May of 2007. They'll be playing in a brand-new stadium that's been a hit beyond Simmons's expectations; the eight luxury suites he originally

planned on building sold out immediately, so he added six more--
and those are also now sold out for the entire season.

Tom Dickson of Professional Sports Marketing says there was a
time when you would sell a minor league team and hoped to make
enough money to pay off the debt. Now, if a team is managed properly
and has a fairly new stadium or the chance of getting one, a minor
league baseball franchise can be worth millions of dollars.

WE'LL NEVER KNOW

We'll probably never know how much the Great Lakes Loons franchise
would fetch on the open market, because it will never be up for sale.
Bill Stavropoulos's third major goal in the baseball project was to
make sure the team would always stay in the Midland area. That
was also important to the foundations, Dow Chemical and Dow
Corning, as they promised millions for the baseball project.

The idea was not to create a privately-owned asset that somebody
might decide to leverage someday by selling it or moving it. The
idea was to give a ballpark and a baseball team to the community so
its residents will have a new place for summer fun. The money the
fans spend at the stadium will help finance the team, but any profits
will go back to the community.

One way to ensure that is to set up a corporate structure similar
to an enterprise such as the American Red Cross. When it was
founded, the Michigan Baseball Foundation applied to the Internal

Revenue Service to become a 501(c)(3) non-profit organization. This would make the MBF exempt from paying federal taxes. The Great Lakes Loons and the Dow Diamond will operate just like any other business, but all of the profits will be put back into the surrounding communities. The money could go to little league programs, or schools, or any other endeavor the Michigan Baseball Foundation would like to help.

That sounds fairly simple, but the process of getting the IRS to sign off on a baseball team's becoming a 501(c)(3) non-profit organization has proved to be an agonizing experience for all concerned.

JUMPING THROUGH HOOPS

For one thing, there's precedent for this idea. The Memphis Redbirds, the Triple A affiliate of the St. Louis Cardinals, operates as a non-profit entity. The Internal Revenue Service signed off on the Memphis Redbirds Foundation operating as a 501(c)(3) non-profit in 1998; businessman Dean Jernigan's goal, when he purchased the team, was to make sure it stayed in Memphis, a city that has seen its share of professional sports teams pick up and leave. He would sell the team to the foundation, the board of which would be made up of volunteers, and the team and the stadium would be run by a management group. No single person or company would make any money from the operation of the ball club or the stadium.

So far, so good; the IRS said yes. Then tax-exempt bonds worth $72 million were sold for the construction of the ballpark; the idea was that the bond money would be paid back by the foundation from the operations of the stadium. At this point, the IRS balked, claiming that the Cardinals, a profit-making entity, would benefit from the proposed stadium. About three years later, a settlement was reached under the terms of which the Memphis Redbirds Foundation paid the IRS $1.6 million, but retained its status as a 501(c)(3) non-profit.

In the midst of all this, someone at the IRS made the comment that the agency would never again grant that kind of nonprofit status to a professional sports team—and, in fact, as of this writing it looks possible that the Michigan Baseball Foundation's request may be denied. A number of other corporate structures are under consideration; no matter how the team and the stadium are eventually set up, it will be in such a way that the primary goals of keeping the team in Midland and returning as much as possible to the community are carried out.

CHAPTER *13*

THE THAW

Spring is coming to central Michigan. It's not here yet—as I write this, it's 28 degrees and snowing—but it's on its way. They're still working on the Dow Diamond. According to Fred Eddy and John Swantek, they'll be putting the finishing touches on it all the way up to opening night. Meanwhile, the Loons are a solid hit; the stands will be packed with fans to cheer them the first time they take the field.

We've been hungry for this. Never before have so many looked forward so eagerly to a Friday the 13th. Not around here, anyway. Somewhere around fifty-three hundred people will converge on the Dow Diamond to watch a lot more than a baseball game. Fifty-three hundred people, maybe more, will have a front-row seat to change.

One thing that will change will be some of our habits on spring and summer nights. We'll still enjoy picnics and barbecues, trips to the beach, and the movies, but now, we'll have another option. We can go to a professional baseball game. Take the whole family. Have a great time.

NOT JUST A GAME

And baseball's just the beginning of it. Dow Chemical, Dow Corning, and Hemlock Semiconductor will draw executives from other companies there, companies they do business with. We hope they'll go to a game at the Dow Diamond and say, "Wow, this ballpark is fantastic. What else have you got around here?"

They'll learn that just fifteen minutes east of here is Bay City, with one big summer event after another. It sits along Saginaw Bay, where boaters and watercraft users enjoy one of the state's greatest resources. Oh, and by the way, you know that property in Bay City where a baseball stadium was once proposed? They're planning to put a Maritime Heritage Center there, which could spur more development along the Saginaw River.

Just ten miles south of Bay City is Saginaw, home to the Ontario Hockey League's Saginaw Spirit, one of the more successful franchises in the OHL. Saginaw is also becoming known for specialized medical procedures and has well-respected health care facilities, such as Covenant HealthCare and St. Mary's of Michigan. Then there's Saginaw Valley State University, which seems to break enrollment records year after year. Delta College is in Bay County, and Northwood

University, an internationally known business school, is right here in Midland. To the west of Midland is Mt. Pleasant, home of Central Michigan University, which also has very high enrollment levels, and also one of the biggest casinos in the state, another entertainment possibility.

They'll see that this is a pretty neat part of the country. It may have been struggling in this new "world order" economy—it's still struggling, as a matter of fact—but in terms of people and education and attractions and natural beauty, it has an awful lot to offer. So the Loons aren't just a baseball team. They're a spark for the region.

NEW HOPE

And what about us? The ones that get up every morning to go to work, hoping that our jobs are secure, hoping that this economic funk we are in will magically disappear? They're a spark for us, too. The day the Dow Diamond hosts its first game will be a new day for the town and for the region.

Now this is not the Field of Dreams, and a ballpark isn't magic. It's not enough, all by itself, to heal the bruises that have befallen this gorgeous part of the country. But it sure is a start. It's a great thing for us, and on behalf of everybody who lives here and loves central Michigan and loves baseball, I just want to say two words to Bill Stavropoulos and all the men and women he knew he could turn to and count on to get this project completed: Thank you.

APPENDIX.
THE MIDWEST LEAGUE

There are about 170 teams in the organization that is called Minor League Baseball. Those 170 teams are in 19 leagues spread across the country. (Again, all of these teams are affiliated with a team in Major League Baseball. There are Independent minor league baseball teams as well, such as the ones in Traverse City and Kalamazoo.)

The Great Lakes Loons are one of 14 teams in the Midwest League of Minor League Baseball and in fact a visitor to the Dow Diamond this season will be George Spelius, the President of the Midwest League. (If you should call the league offices in Beloit, Wisconsin, expect George to answer the phone from time to time. It's that kind of organization.)

Spelius says the owners of the teams in the Midwest League were excited when they heard the group from Midland was pursuing the Battle Creek club. That team was always talking about moving from southwest Michigan because of poor attendance, and he says that in minor league baseball, you can't just break even. You have to have cash flow to be a successful operation and he expects that in Midland. As far as putting the deal together so quickly, Spelius says the Midland group is made up of business people, and they knew how to "push the right buttons."

The Loons will be in the Eastern Division of the Midwest League, which has six teams. There are eight teams in the Western Division of the league, and the reason there are more in that division is that all those teams are west of Chicago.

The Lansing Lugnuts and the West Michigan Whitecaps are the other two Michigan teams in the Midwest League. The Fort Wayne Wizards are also in the Eastern Divison. The team was sold in 2006 by General Sports and Entertainment in Rochester, Michigan. One of the investors in the team was Dick Garber, owner of the Saginaw Spirit hockey team. The Wizards were sold to a company called Hardball Capital. The big talk in Fort Wayne as the 2007 season begins is the possibility of building a brand new, $30 million dollar ballpark in the downtown area. The stadium would be built with public and private funds, and would be part of a $125 million dollar development project for downtown Fort Wayne. Sound familiar?

The Dayton Dragons is the flagship team of the Midwest League, with seven straight years of sellouts at its new stadium, which opened in 2000. In 2006, the Dragons ranked 8th in attendance in all of Minor League Baseball.

The South Bend Silver Hawks round out the Eastern Division. Its funny that South Bend would be the Loons first ever opponent, because the Silver Hawks almost moved to Marion, Illinois, which would have

THE MIDWEST LEAGUE

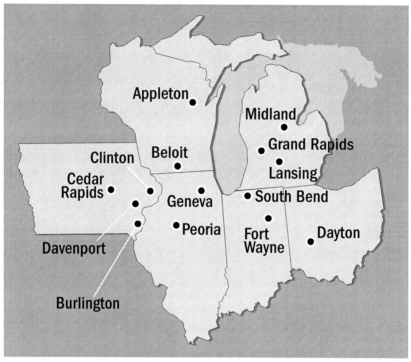

paved the way for the Battle Creek team to move to South Bend, and if that would have happened, April 13th, 2007, would have been just another typical Friday in mid-Michigan.

On to the western division, where the Beloit Snappers could be the next Southwest Michigan Devil Rays. Beloit is located in south central Wisconsin, very close to the Illinois border. Late in 2006, a deal where a new stadium would be built near Beloit fell through, which could force the owners of the team to move or sell the team to someone else. The Snappers play in Pohlman Field, which is one of oldest ballparks in the Midwest League and Beloit drew a little more than 84,000 fans in 2006, next to last in the league.

In central Wisconsin, the Wisconsin Timber Rattlers play in Fox Cities Stadium in Grand Chute, which is near Appleton. That ballpark was built in 1994, and the Timber Rattlers got their name when a marketing firm selected several possibilities, school children then voted on them and Timber Rattlers won out. According to the team's website, the Timber Rattlers are a non-stock community-owned team similar in structure to the Green Bay Packers.

The Kane County Cougars are based in Geneva, Illinois. They moved their from Wausau, Wisconsin in 1991 when they began plan at Elfstrom Stadium, which was designed by HOK Sport, the same firm that drew up the plans for the Dow Diamond. Kane County ranked 19th in attendance in all of minor league baseball.

Also in Illinois, the Peoria Chiefs, who moved into a brand new stadium in 2002. May 24th, 2002 to be exact, and the team recorded many firsts that day, including the first beer bought at the stadium. Greg Sholty has that distinction, and I will dedicate my first beer at the Dow Diamond to him.

In Clinton Iowa, which is right along the border of Illinois, you will find the Clinton Lumberkings. With Lumberkings and Timber Rattlers, I'm glad the Michigan Baseball Foundation steered away from Lumbermen as a nickname. That's too much wood.

The Cedar Rapids Kernels in Cedar Rapids, Iowa play in Veterans Memorial Stadium, which opened in 2002. Voters there approved a referendum to build a new ballpark in 2000, so the old Vet's Stadium was torn down, and now the new one, complete with luxury suites, is now one of the best in the Midwest League.

The Bees reside in Burlington, Iowa. The team plays at Community Field which was built in 1947, but has gone through a number of renovations since then, including a $3 million dollar face-lift in 2005.

Finally, we have the Swing of the Quad Cities in Davenport, Iowa. The team will most likely have new owners starting in 2007 and the ownership group may sound familiar. David Heller, along with business partner Bob Herrfeldt, who make up Main Street Baseball, have purchased the Quad Cities team and the sale was pending for approval by the league. It was Heller who wanted to bring a baseball team to Bay City. While he wasn't able to pull off that deal, he is now an owner of a team in the Midwest League. And in a bit of a twist, Heller's Columbus Catfish in the South Atlantic League is now affiliated with the Tampa Bay Devil Rays, who were affiliated with the team in Battle Creek. The Catfish were affiliated with the Los Angeles Dodgers, who now are with the Great Lakes Loons. As Buck Murdoch of the great "Airplane" movies once said, "Irony can be pretty ironic sometimes."

ACKNOWLEDGEMENTS

Thanks to all the people I interviewed to put this book together, including William Stavropoulos and Michael Hayes of the Michigan Baseball Foundation. Thanks to WJRT-TV General Manager Tom Bryson, News Director Jim Bleicher, and Assistant News Director Jayne Hodak for letting me pursue this project, and allowing me to use the pictures taken from our video stories. Also thanks to the MBF, the Dow Chemical Company and Jeff Glenn Photography for the use of their pictures. Special thanks to Peter Johnston of Foxhound Enterprises, who was given a manuscript in January, copy edited the material, and guided it through the publishing process. If I hadn't got in touch with Peter, this would have never been completed by April 13th. Thanks to my brother-in-law, Joe O'Mara, for his support; to my sister, Pam Theisen, and brother, Steve Camp, for the kind, motivating words, and to my parents, Robert and Gisela Camp, for being role models in what has become my most important job in my life: being a parent.